PRAYERS
FOR
PEOPLE IN
HOSPITAL

NEVILLE SMITH

D0503435

OXFORD UNIVERSITY PRESS
1994

Oxford University Press, Walton Street, Oxford OX2 6DP

Oxford New York Toronto
Delhi Bombay Calcutta Madras Karachi
Kuala Lumpur Singapore Hong Kong Tokyo
Nairobi Das es Salaam Cape Town
Melbourne Auckland Madrid

and associated companies in
Berlin Ibadan

Oxford is a trade mark of Oxford University Press

Published in the United States
by Oxford University Press Inc., New York

© Oxford University Press 1994

ISBN 0 19 110009 9

First published 1994

British Library Cataloguing in Publication Data
Data available

Library of Congress Cataloging in Publication Data
Data available

1 3 5 7 9 10 8 6 4 2

Typeset by Pure Tech Corporation, Pondicherry, India
Printed in Great Britain
on acid-free paper by
Biddles Ltd, Guildford, Surrey

FOREWORD ▨

W HEN I was invited to write a foreword to *Prayers for People in Hospital* I found myself thinking, 'Oh no, not another book of prayers! There are thousands of them already.' Nevertheless, I agreed to do so, though at that time I had not seen the typescript. What a wise decision that proved to be. For, having read it, I feel privileged to be associated with what is an inspiring, informative, and, in many ways, a unique book.

One of the secrets of prayer, especially prayer for others, is knowledge and understanding of the person or situation in question. Our prayers, if they are to be offered with integrity, need to be informed. In this beautifully written book the world of the hospital is sensitively opened up to us. Here are human stories interwoven with perceptive prayers that spring from a depth of sympathetic awareness of the needs of patients and those who visit them. Here also are superb and perceptive insights into the needs of all who work in hospitals. Here is practical wisdom that comes, not from distant theory, but from years spent 'alongside' people in hospital.

Some years ago I was suddenly rushed into hospital with a very serious illness. That experience transformed my attitude towards praying for people in hospital. I believe this book will do the same for its readers. It will open the eyes and inform the mind. It will prove to be a rich resource for those who wish to find suitable prayers to use either in public or in private. But, above all, it will enrich our life of prayer by drawing us closer to those who suffer and those who care for them or, to put it another way, it will enable us to walk in the footsteps of the one known as 'the Wounded Healer'.

The Right Reverend Roy Williamson
Bishop of Southwark

ACKNOWLEDGEMENTS ◈

THIS book has been a long time in the writing. No doubt, looking back, that has been all to the good, otherwise I would not have been able to draw on my experience, as I have done, of working at Guy's Hospital. That experience has been formative in every way, despite the fact that it has come late in my ministry.

My thanks are due to Dick Douglas, formerly of Oxford University Press, who conceived the idea that OUP should produce a successor to *A Hospital Prayer Book*, discussed it with me, and invited me to write it. Nigel Lynn, his successor, has prodded me firmly but gently over a long period into getting the writing done. It has been important to me that he has set achievable deadlines. I have managed to achieve them, but at the expense of my free time, which has always been at a premium since I have worked at Guy's. I acknowledge with gratitude the affectionate tolerance of my wife Anne, during the hours when I have been immured, writing yet another section, still more prayers. In many ways the book has grown and seemed to take on a life of its own.

Some of the sections I could not have completed without the insight and experience of hospital staff—Gill Aston, Paul Carter, and Vera Wootten amongst many others. Trevor Philpott, who was himself a patient, has allowed me to use words which he spoke at the memorial service of the surgeon who operated on him. Julia Caprara was at the bedside of her husband after he had undergone a similar operation, and has agreed to my using some words which she wrote then.

The person to whom my main debt of gratitude is due is Lisa Anderson. She has deciphered my bad cursive handwriting and turned it into typescript. She has been patient with my alterations to the text, and requests to type 'just one more section' when the end had seemed to be in sight.

Finally, my thanks are due to the patients and staff at Guy's around whose experiences I have written so many sections of this book, and formulated the prayers. In virtually all the instances I mention, I have changed names and blurred details to preserve the anonymity of the people concerned. Without them, the book would not have reached its shape, or perhaps even have taken shape at all.

Alternative Service Book, 'Collect of Good Friday', from the *Alternative Service Book*, © 1980 The Central Board of Finance of the Church of England.

London Committee of Licensed Teachers of Anatomy, for permission to use an adapted form of the 'Ecumenical Service of Thanksgiving'.

Biblical quotations are from **The Revised English Bible**, © 1989 by permission of Oxford and Cambridge University Presses.

Society for Promoting Christian Knowledge; Bishop Michael Ramsey, from *Through the Year with Michael Ramsey*, ed. Margaret Duggan (1975); Keith Ward, from *The Living God* (1984). Used by permission of the publishers.

Fount, an imprint of **Harper Collins Publishers Limited**; Margaret Spufford, from *Celebration* (1989).

CONTENTS ▨

INTRODUCTION ▣

Prayers for People in Hospital was conceived as a replacement for *A Hospital Prayer Book*, first published by Oxford University Press in 1933. That book was originally compiled for the Wingfield–Morris Orthopaedic Hospital, Oxford, by the Revd (later Bishop) David Porter, vicar at that time of All Saints', Highfield, and chaplain to the hospital. In its OUP format, it went through several editions until its final booklet form of 1959 when its selling price was two shillings and sixpence ($12\frac{1}{2}$p).

The foreword was written by an anonymous member of the consultant staff who signed himself simply 'FRCS'. However it was not entirely clear from the foreword or the contents whether the booklet was intended for use by patients or members of staff. Perhaps the merit of the book was that it was capable of being used by both. Prayers were provided which could be used within a suggested framework of personal devotion. Additionally, from the annotated copy which I found on one of the wards at Guy's, it is clear that *A Hospital Prayer Book* was used as a source for leading prayer in the morning and evening at a time when ward prayers formed part of the daily routine.

By contrast, *Prayers for People in Hospital* is not intended to be used in hospital. There exist any number of well-produced books, pamphlets, and prayer cards which set out prayers for people to use while they are ill in hospital, and a selection of biblical texts which they may find helpful. The intention of this book is not to add to that number.

Nor is it to provide prayers or prayer material for hospital chaplains. They know their own hospitals, the situations which are important within them, the needs of the hospital staff, and the patients whom they serve. Chaplains will bring these areas of concern before God in their own prayers which will vary according to their theological outlook and understanding, and their own spirituality.

Prayers for People in Hospital is intended for use by people outside hospital who want to pray for people inside. As far as I am aware, there is no other book which specifically seeks to help people to do this. Usually, patients are the primary concern of our prayers, and on the face of it their needs are obvious—that they should make a good recovery from their illness as soon as possible. However, patients' real needs may be less apparent. I have tried, therefore, to focus on some of those areas that have an equal claim to be the attention of our prayers but which it is easy to overlook; for example, patients' fears and anxieties, their rights to privacy and space, the long periods of waiting and boredom which they may have to endure. I have also provided prayers about people in areas of hospital care and treatment which some may find difficult to pray for, since moral overtones are inevitably present: termination of pregnancy; HIV and AIDS; drug dependency, and alcohol abuse. No doubt the pictures I have drawn, or the colours in which I have described them, will communicate something of my own feelings, and these will be articulated in the prayers I have framed. I am aware of the psycho-social reasons which may play their part in bringing people into hospital for treatment in these areas, but I am also aware of human responsibility. I believe in a loving, caring, forgiving God, and the vulnerability shown in the living and dying of Jesus Christ, but I am also aware of human frailty. I often feel angry with God at the apparent injustices which people suffer in their lives and to which I can find no answer. Anger in itself can be a form of prayer, and as such I acknowledge it. It is part of me. But my anger passes into sadness, and it is this more lasting feeling which will probably be detected in my prayers in response to the situations in which people find themselves in hospital. Some of those that I describe had a happy outcome. Many did not. All of them touched on my own vulnerability. I have included them in order to build up an overall picture of hospital life.

Very few people are completely alone in the world, so one

person's admission to hospital usually has a 'ripple' effect on numerous people, from close family to friends and acquaintances. They, too, with their needs and anxieties, are 'people in hospital' who need our prayers.

Because of the emotive appeal of people who are ill, it is easy to overlook the fact that most of the people in hospital are staff, not patients. Hospitals employ a wide range of people from cleaners and chaplains to consultants in a wide range of specialties. Guy's, for example, has something like 800 beds and 3,000 members of staff. Each of them has a function to perform which is vital to the smooth and efficient running of the hospital as an institution, and to the quality of care which it ultimately delivers to the patient at the bedside.

Yet this wider aspect of hospital life is often ignored or forgotten. I recently received a mailing which included a prayer for hospitals. It asked God to 'Bless doctors, nurses, and orderlies'. Orderlies disappeared from the hospital scene long ago, and whilst doctors and nurses provide the most obvious face of hospital care, they could not perform their work without the support and co-operation of many other members of staff spread throughout the hospital, many of whom will never have any contact with the patients themselves. These unseen members of staff are often under greater pressure than the patients whom they are serving and they, no less than the patients, deserve to be the subject of our prayers. This book, therefore, has a comprehensive title. The 'people in hospital', for whom our prayers are offered, are staff as well as patients, their families and friends. My intention is that we should be able to pray for them with insight and understanding.

I hope also that people will be enabled to pray imaginatively. The situations are mine, the prayers are mine, and the style in which they are expressed is mine. It can be no other. I visited recently an exhibition of paintings by a number of different artists. The style of each group of paintings was unmistakably the same and bore the mark of the individual artist. So with the prayers in this book. Some people may want to use them as they are. Others may want to adapt them to their own particular circumstances.

Others still may simply want to use them as a resource. Any of these approaches would be in line with my own aims in compiling this book.

My intention also is that the prayers in this book should be used constructively by those who lead worship in our churches. Some people may choose to use them as they stand as part of the prayers of intercession during the service. Others may want to use them as a source of material for intercession during the Eucharist. Those who lead house-groups, prayer-meetings, Bible-study groups, services of healing, may choose to use the illustrative material and the prayers in a quieter and more reflective way. I hope also that the book will be of use to people who want to say their own prayers, include in them the needs of the sick, and those who look after them, but who may not know what to pray for and find it difficult to frame their prayers in any structured or ordered way. I hope that by using this book they too will feel that they are entering into hospital life and contributing to it their own ministry of prayer and intercession.

My aim, therefore, is to draw a picture, or series of pictures of hospital life. I hope that those who want to pray will feel that they are entering into it, and that they can understand the needs of the people involved, patients, relatives, and staff alike. In that way they are joining in God's healing process as they offer their prayers for people in hospital.

PRAYING FOR PEOPLE IN HOSPITAL ▨

A FEW days before I wrote these words, I had taken the funeral of an attractive young woman who had died of cancer. She had fought the illness long and bravely, and I had got to know her and her husband well. As I stood at the crematorium waiting for the hearse to arrive, I remembered other funerals at which I had officiated there. There was a young man with a wife and teenage children who had died after a long battle against cancer. Another man of about the same age with a similar family had died after an even longer history of renal failure. I remembered taking the funeral of triplets who had died very shortly after birth, and the haunting sight of three tiny coffins lined up together on the catafalque (the crematorium had sympathetically relaxed its rule of individual committal and I was able to commit all three babes together). I had prayed for all these people at some stage of their illness, with the exception of two of the triplets who had died a matter of minutes after they were born, and before I was called. Nevertheless I had baptized the third, and in using the Lord's Prayer at his baptism, I had prayed 'thy will be done'. How, I thought as I stood there on a grey afternoon in late September, could I come to terms with the sad chapter of memories that the crematorium evoked within me? Could it be that God had not heard my prayer, or that he had chosen to reject my prayer?

These questions led me to reflect on my belief in God and to consider once more the purpose of intercessory prayer in his scheme of things. We are often urged to pray for other people. What are we actually doing? If prayer works, how does it work?

I sought an answer from the books on my shelves. I turned first to Bishop Michael Ramsey who ordained me, and has always been a source of good sense and sound spirituality through his writings. I found these words:

How do we co-operate with God's good purpose towards the world? Partly by our actions, which are a channel of God's purpose, and partly by our prayers, which are also a channel of God's purpose . . . And we best do it if we first and foremost put ourselves in touch with the great stream of God's loving purpose and become channels in his name, irrigating the parched desert of a world saddened, divided, sinful and estranged. (*Through the Year with Michael Ramsey*, ed. Margaret Duggan, SPCK, 1975)

Searching further, I found words from a rather different background but which are remarkably similar in their approach.

If we are seriously concerned to see how God's purpose may be better realised in the world, and if, in that context, we bring our concerns for others into our thoughts, then it may well be—and I believe it will be—that our prayers enter into the determining nexus of causality. That is, they become positive influences upon the way things go. They play a part in the creation of the future, because God weaves them, with all the other factors of natural causality and human free actions and his own purposes, into the pattern of the developing world. All our prayers are used. They influence the future for good. But we cannot say how they may be used, since we have no idea at all of what other constraints there are upon the determination of the future.

So we may certainly pray for others and we may expect God to use (a better word than 'answer') our prayers. (Keith Ward, *The Living God*, SPCK, 1984)

In both these quotations, the writers are developing Jesus' own teaching about prayer as we find it recorded in the Gospels. 'Ask and you will receive,' says Jesus, 'seek and you will find, knock and the door will be opened' (Luke 1: 9). These words are echoed later in the Gospel where Luke records the parable of the widow and the judge: 'Will not God give justice to his chosen, to whom he listens patiently while they cry out to him day and night?' (Luke 18: 7). The question is rhetorical and demands the answer 'yes'. In many situations, however, the opposite seems to be the case. God, it seems, cannot be relied on to 'give justice to his chosen . . . while they cry out to him day and night'. One such situation is illness. This is a frequent source of real difficulty for Christian people, even those with a deep commitment. I have known people who have spent hours at the bedside of a loved one praying hard all the time for recovery, but with no effect. I have known patients who have been surrounded by the prayers of people in their churches, and in groups all over the world, but who have not made the recovery that was prayed for. So people experience a sense of failure. Either the faith which they profess has let them down at a time when it most mattered, or, more probably, they have been found lacking in faith when a time of crisis arrived. Either way, their own prayer and the prayer of those around them has not produced the desired effect at the moment of their greatest need. Their experience, therefore, has not been a happy one and this has served to reinforce the impact of their illness upon them.

Another quotation from Michael Ramsey is apposite at this point.

So many people think of prayer as a kind of bombardment . . . But it is a wrong idea about God and about praying, for two reasons. First it suggests that God is somewhere rather far away and has to be reached by a kind of spiritual heavy artillery. And secondly because it suggests that prayer is something we start with our own little ideas and requests. No, if God is Creator, Father, Friend, the Lover of Mankind, the real point about prayer is being in touch with him like the touch of human friendship; enjoying his presence and being near to him, so that a great deal passes from us to him and from him to us in a happy, joyful—though sometimes painful—intercourse . . . The words you exchange are only a small part of what is exchanged simply by presence and happiness and the mutual impact of person upon person. (*Through the Year with Michael Ramsey*, ed. Margaret Duggan, SPCK, 1975)

These last words echo the experiences of many people who feel themselves supported in their illness. At a time when they are unable to pray for themselves they are upheld by the prayers of their fellow Christians. I know this was my feeling when I underwent an operation recently. It was a satisfying and fulfilling experience which I can only describe as healing. I ask myself if I would have felt the same if the outcome of the operation had not been successful. I believe I would since the prayer which Michael Ramsey describes is beyond words—'a great deal passes from us to him . . . and the mutual impact of person upon person'.

However, his words earlier in this quotation encapsulate the age-long question about people who do not make a physical recovery, and are not healed in themselves. He speaks of God as 'Creator, Father, Friend, the Lover of Mankind'. If these attributes are true, as we believe, we are faced with the problem of holding them in tension with pain and illness, suffering and death. How can God, as we believe him to be, coexist with tragedy as we know it to be?

Of one thing I am certain. God does not send affliction on his people in order to test them, as happened in the story of Job. If God knows us, our reaction to adversity is already clear to him. Some of us will cope badly. In others it will bring out the best. There is a belief which I hear expressed sometimes that suffering bravely borne can be an inspiration to other people and therefore ennobles both the sufferer and those who look after them. I recognize that this can be true. Some people may rise above their illness in a way which indicates that they are sharing the existential life of the risen and living Christ. Nevertheless, I remain profoundly uneasy with any suggestion that God should allow illness or deliberately bring about a situation in order for his chosen ones to show their mettle, triumph over adversity, and bring out the best in other people. The passion narratives seem to point in the other direction. The suffering of Jesus and his impending death did not inspire the disciples to respond in his time of need. They slept while he prayed in the Garden of Gethsemane. They all forsook him and fled when he was arrested. Peter denied three times that he knew Jesus. When Jesus died on the cross, there were only two or three of his own people with him. The others watched from a distance.

Nor am I happy with the example of Job. I have never been comfortable with the last chapter of that book where God speaks to him from the whirlwind and tells him that there are things which he cannot understand and never will. Job is able to accept this, and we share his acceptance when we stand before the great mysteries of life and death. Nevertheless God has given us our intellect, and in every other area of life we use our powers of intelligence to try to make sense of life as we know it, including those things which are apparently closed to us.

Margaret Spufford, whom I came to know briefly when her daughter Bridget was in Guy's towards the end of her life, grapples with this problem in her book *Celebration* (Fount, 1989). In a powerful and moving chapter on 'Prayer and Pain', she works through 'the irreconcilable clashes in my life between human experience and what I am bound to believe' (p. 80). She continues: 'One of the most helpful things that was ever said to me was "The definition of 'Almighty' means that there is no evil out of which good cannot be brought". This I have found, extremely painfully, to be true. The fundamentally awry can perhaps never be made whole in this life; yet like the twisted tree, or the child's courage and wisdom, it can take on a beauty of its own. And in this transformation, the constant presence of an enabling God seems to me vital. My image of a Creator in whose creation there are mistakes not logically comprehensible may be true, but it has to be extended into the image of a Creator who ceaselessly, patiently, works to transform and re-create what has gone amiss, above all in His own entry into this creation to amend and redeem it. Some of this re-creation and patient transformation of what has gone amiss I can myself bear witness to. But if those theologians who assert that God is in total control of His creation are right, I cannot worship Him. Integrity demands that I do hand in my ticket. For I still cannot cope with the endemic nature of pain. And integrity has to come higher than anything else at all, even God, or at least my present perception of Him.'

I, too, feel that I must at all costs preserve that integrity in the situations in which I am called upon to pray with people. This can be especially difficult when a patient is obviously dying and I am asked to pray for recovery. I cannot refuse to pray—but I must know what I am praying for. It cannot be for recovery because I cannot realistically pray that natural processes should be set aside or reversed. I have seen enough dying people to know when the onset of death is irreversible.

Also, if I pray for recovery when death is imminent, I am not helping my friends and colleagues on the hospital staff. For them, the death of a patient is never easy, and my prayer will do nothing to relieve the situation or make death go away. I must maintain the integrity of my ministry towards them—as I must towards the family and relatives.

To pray for recovery, as they requested, may not be the kindest or the most loving response to their needs. To do so may only encourage them to cling on to their loved one when it would be more helpful for them to be able to let go. The realities of the situation have to be faced and talked about before any meaningful prayer is possible. To arrive, and launch into a series of set or stereotyped prayers is meaningless and unhelpful. It is also insensitive and virtually insulting to the family concerned, not valuing them as people in need. The situation has to be pastorally explored, then, when the time comes, I would want to pray for healing, peace, and acceptance. The three, inevitably, merge closely into each other.

I believe it is always possible to pray for healing, whatever the situation. Healing, unfortunately, has become synonymous in many Church circles with cure or recovery. It is beyond the scope of this chapter to pursue this in depth, and I must content myself with an expression of regret in passing. For our purposes, healing means people being put back together even within the trauma which they have experienced, finding resources within themselves which they hardly knew existed, finding God's presence with them, experiencing his love and acceptance, and therefore his peace. This is healing—being made whole. It is significant that the two words—heal, whole—both derive from the same word in old English.

For the dying patient, it may be that death will bring the only healing possible. There is no better prayer we can offer than that our loved one will be kept in God's presence, in his love, and therefore find peace. Bereaved families have said to me so many times that their relative looked so much more peaceful in death. This I believe is true, rather than just wishful thinking to give them a shred of comfort at a time of great distress.

All this involves acceptance. For me, acceptance is the foundation of all my prayers for people in hospital. But first, it is important to consider what acceptance means, what it includes, and what it excludes. The latter is perhaps more easily dealt with.

Acceptance can so often denote a sad, listless kind of passivity—'there's not much we can do about it, so we shall have to go along with it.' An outward expression of this is the inscription 'Thy will be done' on countless headstones. We have already thought about the theological difficulty of this phrase in relation to illness and death. On an emotional level, it probably blankets the painful protest against lives cut short by premature and unexpected death. In this sense, 'acceptance' has become debased.

In total contrast, I want to use acceptance as a positive quality. It is a quality which contains within it an outward-going movement which enables a person to enhance both their own life and the lives of others with whom they come into contact. Most of us, I am sure, will know people who fit this description. They have qualities which transcend illness, handicap, even death itself.

Because they have accepted themselves and their situation, they are able to live through it, and encourage others to do the same. They are able to experience 'life in all its fullness'—the gift of God himself. My prayer is that people should be able to do that, even when they are ill or dying, even when they are anxious for those whom they love, even when they are tired and stressed from looking after others. All of them are 'people in hospital'. Acceptance is the key. How, then, do we perceive or experience acceptance so that it may become the basis of our prayers?

Acceptance is above all realistic—and we need to be realistic in order to come to terms with what is happening, or has happened, to us. When things are bad, we instinctively push them away. There is something within us that does not want to believe they have happened. Perhaps it is a sort of anaesthetic quality. People often feel that events have a kind of nightmare quality. They feel that they will wake up to find that all the bad things were unreal and that they have now disappeared. I have no magic wand, as a minister, to make things come right. Sometimes my sense of inadequacy is such that I wish I had. I also know that sometimes I am regarded as the man who is brought in to work a much-needed miracle. All I can do is to help people in a way which they may least want, but most need: to be realistic about the situation in which they find themselves, and enable them to find some degree of acceptance. To pray with them is part of this. I cannot pray that the moment and all that it involves will pass. But I can and do pray that people will be able to face the situation realistically, accept it, and find strength to deal with it. So often they do. It is remarkable how people find deep within themselves springs of untapped resourcefulness and unexpected strength.

This turn of phrase brings to mind the imagery of Psalm 23. The shepherd leads the sheep to green pasture and to water where they may lie down and rest. And people are able to rest because, having faced reality, they are at peace with themselves and the world. Even if they should 'walk through a valley of deepest darkness' they would fear no harm because God is with them. They have faced the pain of loss and separation involved in illness and/or death, and in accepting it, have overcome its power.

In Alan Ayckbourn's play, *Just between Ourselves*, Dennis sits lightly to all the difficulties and complications which bedevil the relationships between his wife and his mother who lives with them, and which form the context in which he lives his life. His approach is that he can either laugh them away or by laughing sufficiently, can convince himself that the difficulties do not even exist. Needless to say, the play hinges on the dire consequences of his refusal to accept the events of life as they are played out around him.

This is very different from the positive acceptance of the pain of relationships or illness or death. It is still possible to laugh or go on laughing, but only when the pain has been accepted or absorbed. This can only be done by setting it within the context of human love and friendship, a context in which Christians believe God is active and at work.

The person who prays, therefore, must do so in terms which are relevant and meaningful for those on whose behalf the prayers are offered. The minister is, in a sense, acting as their advocate before God. It is important, therefore, that we should do our best to pray from where other people are, not from where we are ourselves. In other words, our prayer should, as far as possible, represent the outlook and ideas of the people on whose behalf we are standing before God at that moment. Obviously, this can be difficult. It is not easy, with only a brief acquaintance, to get inside the minds and thought-forms of other people and appreciate their world-view. People may have little or no religious background and their outlook may be widely separated from that of the mainstream Churches. It may be difficult to bridge the gap. We shall therefore find ourselves praying very simply and informally—but none the worse for that.

A colleague with whom I discussed this question would want to go further. His practice is to offer prayers in the words that patients and their families have used themselves. This means he includes their anger, abuse, and even blasphemy. I appreciate his reasons for doing this, and the theological justification for it. I can only say that for myself, I would not be comfortable with this outspoken method of prayer, however realistic it may be.

No matter how bad the situation may be, there are almost always reasons for which it is possible to give thanks in prayer. The care and attention provided by the hospital staff is one good reason. Another is the relationship which the person who is ill enjoys, or has enjoyed, with their family. Even though death may be approaching, family ties are still precious, especially surrounded by the many memories gathered over the years. Obviously circumstances of illness and death vary from person to person, as do the quality of relationships within families. Nevertheless, it is realistic to include thanksgiving in our prayers for people who are ill and their relatives. Such prayers can have a cathartic effect and enable both patients and families, in looking back, also to look forward, and to face the situation in which they find themselves with openness and acceptance.

This is, in fact, another way of describing the Christian experience of death and resurrection. I want people to know that where they are, Christ has been before, and is already. He has hung upon the cross and uttered the cry of dereliction: 'My God, my God, why have you forsaken me?' (Psalm 22: 1). Many patients and families make this prayer their own when they are confronted with their own personal crisis, and try to make sense of the mysteries of life and death, pain, and illness. The good things of life are equally mysterious, yet we seem not to ponder so much on them—art, music, beauty, joy, happiness. To be able to experience these qualities means that we are able to experience hurt. To be sensitive enough to be able to rejoice in the good things makes us sensitive to those that are painful.

Jesus' prayer on the cross is one which I, in my own way, enter into. There are times when I come from the wards and simply stand in the chapel in bewilderment. I can hardly believe that people can go through the circumstances, whether physical, emotional, or social, in which I have found them, and tried to minister to them, and still survive. My prayer is that as they share the experience of pain and desolation, so they may also share the experience of resurrection. Many of us will know people whose experience fits this description. I have a favourite story which illustrates the point well. Even though it is not about people, it stands as a parable.

When I was in Lancaster, a job-creation scheme turned a small, derelict corner of the old city into a pleasant sitting-out area, complete with a bench, flower-bed, and ornamental tree, planted as a sapling. One day as I passed by, I noticed that vandals had broken the top off the tree and that it was hanging limply down. I wondered what the City Council would do. I wanted them to replace the tree, but the Gardens Department, in its wisdom, did nothing except to cut off the broken top. Next spring, the tree was alive and well, not with one stem, but with two, shooting from where the wound had been.

These are my prayers for patients and relatives. I want to pray realistically also for hospital staff. My prayer for them is that they too should know within themselves the death–resurrection experience even though I am aware that many of them are not Christian, and do not have a mental framework in which Christian imagery is meaningful. Nevertheless, many of them are sensitive and thinking people. They are conscious of the contribution they make through their work to the life of the hospital, and they are equally conscious of the impact that their work has on them. Many of them work under great pressure, and carry the responsibility of making important and far-reaching decisions. Some of these are clinical, with the lives of people at stake, and the well-being of their families. Other decisions are managerial and financial, with large sums of money involved which may affect the lives and livelihood of hospital staff. Some staff are under pressure from dealing with large numbers of people. For others, the pressure may arise from having to meet expectations and deadlines. Many of these experiences are painful. People who work in hospital are inevitably reminded of their own vulnerability. In sharing the pain of others, their own areas of pain are exposed. They are also reminded of their own mortality. In dealing with the death of others, they are reminded of the people that they have known and loved and lost, and that they, too, one day must die. This is the unseen cost of working in hospital. This is the realism underlying the work in which hospital staff engage. My prayer for them must therefore be equally realistic. I pray that they should come through 'the valley of deepest darkness'—however that may be defined for each individual person—to become fuller, deeper, more complete people. My words, I know, inadequately describe the essence of my prayer. I am praying that people who work in hospital should become more whole. I am praying that they, together with the other people in hospital, patients and relatives, should be healed.

PRAYERS FOR PEOPLE IN HOSPITAL

I

AREAS OF HOSPITAL CARE

FAMILIES ⬖

ONE day, I was called to the Intensive Care Unit where a man lay dying. I was told that the family had sent for me to pray for him and give him a blessing. When I arrived it was difficult to know from which part of the family the request had come. The man's young wife was sitting alone in the corridor. His brothers and sisters formed a separate silent group in the relatives' room. From a first glance at the geographical separation of the members of the family it was apparent that all was not well, and that tensions existed within the family relationship.

On another occasion, I called to see the parents of a poorly baby whom I had baptized a few days previously. The mother was busily occupied tending the baby as much as she could, given the amount of high-tech equipment surrounding her. The father was at the other end of the ward reading his newspaper. I talked with him first and he seemed as interested in talking about the events of the day as he did in talking about the progress of his tiny daughter. He was obviously coping with the discouraging news about her by distancing himself, literally as well as metaphorically, from the situation.

Fortunately the couple had a stable relationship, and were able to cope with the stress of the crisis. However, there are some couples who do not, and there is statistical evidence to indicate that serious or prolonged illness in a child can be a crucial factor in the breakdown of some marriages.

**Father,
as your son, our Lord Jesus Christ
hung upon the Cross,
he commended his mother
to the care of the beloved disciple.**

> **Be with all families**
> **in time of their need**
> **especially those**
> **whose relationships are strained,**
> **even to breaking-point,**
> **by the impact of illness upon their lives.**
>
> **Grant to them the gifts of patience**
> **tolerance**
> **compassion**
> **towards those whom they know so well,**
> **and after the pattern of your love in Jesus**
> **may they find understanding, reconciliation, and peace.**

Fortunately, the proximity of death can have the opposite effect. Take the example of Fred, who was in hospital for a number of medical conditions, the most serious of which was cancer of the lung. His wife visited him faithfully and regularly. Usually she was there when I saw him, but one day when we were on our own, he told me that he knew his illness was incurable, and that he would not go home again. 'But this illness has brought me and the wife together,' he said. 'For years we've been passing like ships in the night. She was working days. I was working nights. We hardly ever used to see each other. Now, since I've had this illness, we've got to know each other again, and that's good. We've been able to talk about all kinds of things we haven't discussed for years.'

> **Father,**
> **we give thanks for all**
> **who are able to use the time**
> **you have given them in hospital**
> **to renew family relationships,**
> **to forgive past hurts,**
> **to affirm present affection,**
> **to rediscover gifts of personality**
> **forgotten with the passage of time,**

and to enjoy afresh
the sustenance and nourishment
of mutual acceptance.

May both they and their families
be deepened and upheld
in their love for one another,
and know that their love
is an extension of your love
made known to us
in Jesus, your Son, our Lord.

VISITORS ◈

D AY by day, I see people coming into hospital to visit their
friends and relatives who are patients there. Frequently
they come bearing gifts—flowers, fruit, chocolates, and
sweets. I often think the gifts are unnecessary. People come with the
most valuable gift they have, which is themselves, their time and
energy. Many have come considerable distances and put up with the
inconvenience of London traffic, lack of parking facilities, and the
difficulties of public transport in order to reach the hospital at all.

Difficulties can continue even when they reach the bedside. On
Mothering Sunday, for instance, families had obviously made a
special effort. But at one bedside, a middle-aged woman and her
husband sat by her elderly mother, in silence, the topics of
conversation soon exhausted. The situation was only broken when
the mother herself decided that she needed to visit the toilet. On
another ward, two young men in their twenties sat uncomfortably
with their mother. They had presented their cards and their
flowers but they had nothing else to say. She found protection in
dozing, they passed the time watching the comings and goings and
general activity on the ward. There was no communication
between them.

By contrast, years ago I witnessed on a male surgical ward one of
the best and most expressive examples of hospital visiting. An elderly
woman had come to see her husband, who was sitting up in bed
recovering from his operation. She came into the ward, greeted
him, and caught up on the latest news about his progress. She
gathered up the dirty clothes from his locker, and replaced them
with clean ones. She then sat down in the chair beside his bed. She
took out of her capacious bag the evening paper, which she gave to
her husband to read, and her knitting. There they sat, in silence,

but quite contented, doing in hospital what they obviously did together every evening at home. They were relaxed and comfortable with each other's presence. No words were spoken or needed to be spoken. But real communication was taking place.

Other visitors are frustrated by their inability to communicate with their loved one. They may be unconscious, recovering from an operation, on a life-support machine or simply unable to speak because of illness or the operation they have undergone. Others still wait anxiously while surgery takes place, and time stands still. As one wife said to me later: 'It's only when it's all over that you realize just how anxious you were.'

> Heavenly Father,
> we pray for all
> who come to hospital
> to visit their loved ones:
> those who travel long distances
> those who find the journey tedious
> those who find the visit onerous
> those who come expecting good news
> those who come and find bad news
> those who come with joyful steps
> those who come in fear and anxiety
> those who come with heavy hearts
> those who go on their way rejoicing
> those who leave exhausted by their visit.
>
> As you have been with us,
> and spoken to us
> in Jesus your Son,
> so may we meet one another
> in openness and truth,
> and find strength
> to support in time of need
> in love which binds us together
> and to you
> in Jesus, your Son, our Lord.

ACCIDENT AND EMERGENCY ⬦

N OT long ago, I had the great pleasure of officiating at the
wedding in Guy's Chapel of one of our ward sisters.
The bridegroom was a policeman. They had met when the
bride was working in the Accident and Emergency Department of
another hospital before she moved back to her present post in
Guy's.

'Accident and Emergency' is the most cosmopolitan area of the
hospital. It is also the least predictable. Through its doors flows a
never-ending stream of people from all walks of life, every stratum
of society. There are the local people who come straight to Guy's
rather than go to their GP first. For them Guy's is the community
hospital which its founder intended it to be. Some alcoholics and
drug addicts are regular visitors, but for most people, their arrival
is unplanned and unexpected, and has required the involvement of
the emergency services.

Members of the police and ambulance services are therefore
often to be seen in Accident and Emergency and they get to know
the hospital staff. Their common bond is in sharing the trauma and
anxiety of people whose normal routine of life has suddenly been
interrupted through accident or the onset of sudden illness.
Naturally, stress levels are high. It is demanding to know that the
whole purpose of one's work is to respond swiftly and accurately
to unexpected and unforeseen circumstances.

This is especially true when a Major Incident occurs. At the time
of writing, Guy's has been involved in no less than five over the
previous two years. At such times, members of virtually all
departments are called to the Accident and Emergency Department
to await the arrival of casualties, those who have lost their lives,
and friends and relatives, desperately seeking information and

making enquiries. The moment is all action. Order must be imposed where otherwise there would be chaos. There is no time for talking until the emergency is over and staff have been stood down. Then the trauma will be relived and retold. Each person's vulnerability will have been tested to the utmost. The debriefing will provide some measure of relief but the memories will last much longer. From all the talking, one essential element will emerge and stand clear: the efficient handling of a Major Incident will depend largely on the trust and understanding built up over a period of time between the emergency services and staff in 'A and E'.

Almighty God
Whose will it is
to bring order out of chaos.

We thank you for all who work
in the emergency services
and in the Accident and Emergency departments
of our hospitals.
We thank you for the support
which they bring to people facing the unknown, the unexpected,
and sudden crisis in their lives.

We pray for all who serve
in this area of human care.
Strengthen their trust in each other.
Deepen their respect for one another.
Uphold them in moments of trauma
and in times of lasting stress,
so that they may rest secure in you,
and bring to people in distress
the care and understanding which they need,
after the pattern of your Son,
Jesus Christ our Lord.

PEOPLE UNDERGOING
SURGERY ▨

I WENT to see Georgina on the day before she was to have a
major operation. She had cancer of the throat. Her voice-box
was to be removed, and she would not be able to speak again,
not, at least, in the usual way. This would be a sad loss, for she was
an outward-going and talkative woman.

She was under no illusion as to the seriousness of her condition
or the operation. She had put all her affairs in order, and on the
Sunday before her operation she had asked for a special blessing
upon her and her husband. I was very pleased to be able to do this
and we had a short service together in the day room on the ward,
attended by some of the nursing staff who would be looking after
her. We included a prayer for them in the service.

I went to see her again on the Monday, although everything that
was to be said had been said the previous day. She was not a
religious person and had no Church background, yet I wanted to
give her some final thought that she might hang on to, something
that took her beyond the immediate future involving surgery and
intensive care. For no apparent reason there came into my mind
the words from the opening song of the old Boy Scout Gang
Show:

> We're riding along on the crest of a wave . . .
> We're setting our eyes on
> the distant horizon . . .

It was trite, maybe, but it was where I wanted Georgina to set her
sights. Some old friends came into her room to see her, and talk

with her for the last time. She told them of our conversation and the old words which had come back across the years.

> **Loving Father,**
> **we acknowledge before you**
> **our fear of the unknown,**
> **our hesitancy before the oblivion of anaesthetic,**
> **our desire for life,**
> **and the recovery of health and strength.**
>
> **We pray for those**
> **who are to undergo surgery.**
> **Give them confidence and faith**
> **in the hands of those**
> **to whom they commit themselves,**
> **and who care for them,**
> **so that together they may work**
> **to forward the healing purpose**
> **of your love.**

After the operation, I went to see Georgina again. The operation, serious though it was, had gone well and she nodded her head, as far as the tubes would allow, to acknowledge my presence. I reminded her of our previous conversation. She gave me a warm smile and a 'thumbs-up'. Perhaps my message had got there, after all.

> Heal me, Lord, and I shall be healed,
> save me and I shall be saved;
> for you are my praise.
>
> (Jeremiah 17: 14)

God our Father,
source of all healing and strength
accept our thanksgiving
for all who have successfully
undergone surgery.
We give thanks for the skill
of all those concerned
in their operations,
and of all those who now
continue their treatment.

Give us all thankful hearts
for your goodness towards us,
so that we may dedicate ourselves
again to your service,
and live and work
to your praise and glory.

THE INTENSIVE CARE UNIT:
PATIENTS AND FAMILIES ◈

'INTENSIVE CARE' is a title around which may cluster many
anxieties. Patients on the unit are by definition seriously ill and
their families and friends are anxious about them. Their
anxiety may be heightened by the first sight of the unit: tubes,
drips, wires of every kind connect with monitors which, from time
to time, emit warning signals. The array of machinery is
bewildering and overwhelming. People find it difficult to accept
that the naked body lying there in total passivity is their nearest
and dearest, who is normally fit and active, and with whom they
share their lives.

Conversely, intensive care may convey a message of confidence
and hopefulness. People are reassured by the amount of equipment
brought to bear on the needs of their loved one. They are grateful
both for the 'high-tech', and for the skill and experience with which
it is used. They are grateful above all for the professional
commitment of the hospital staff, and for the support on a personal
level which they extend to families and friends.

This balance between the intensive care unit as a source of
anxiety or reassurance is well captured in the following lines
written by a wife whose husband was in intensive care following
major heart-bypass surgery:

Intensive Care, 11 March 1991

It was as if one was at the centre of the labyrinth—
the tight hold of the vortex—the focus of a radiant
energy of light surrounding a body held only by the
swathes of tubes, connections, and monitors.
I found here, not a land of terror as I had expected
but a place more holy than I had ever met.
A sense of mystery and respect, a focus of calm that
I can only speak of as silent worship.
Love in its most silent but active form.

(Julia Caprara)

—————

**Eternal Father,
we pray for all
whose loved ones are in intensive care.
Be with them in their hopes.
Support them in their anxieties.
Give them sure confidence
in your unfailing presence,
and in your unchanging love;
through Jesus Christ, our Lord.**

INTENSIVE CARE: STAFF ▨

I WAS called yet again to the intensive care unit. On my way, I counted up how many times I had been there during the previous few days, and remarked on this to one of the sisters when I arrived. She agreed that it had been a bad week. Five patients had died during that time, and the one for whom I had been called appeared unlikely to survive. 'The trouble is,' said the sister, 'your feelings begin to get blunted. We give the best possible care to the patients and look after their relatives in every way we possibly can. But you reach a point where you've given all you've got, and there's less and less of yourself in it.'

I knew what she meant. I felt much the same. I had to admit I had had as much as I could take of intensive care for the time being, and did not want to be involved with this latest patient. I would minister to him to the best of my ability and support the relatives in whatever way I could. Probably they would express their appreciation. But I knew that my heart would not be in it. I had been drained by the events of the week, and I felt I had little left to give.

Jesus said to the disciples, 'Come with me . . . and rest a little.' With many coming and going they had no time even to eat.   (Mark 6: 31)

Father,
your Son in his earthly life
knew strain and weariness
through ministering to those
for whom he cared.

Be with those
who bear the responsibility
of working in intensive care.
Prosper their efforts to nurture the life
of those in great need.
Support them in the stress
which decisions of life and death
lay upon them.
And grant them the strength
which they need
to care both for others
and for themselves.
In the name of Jesus Christ, our Lord.

Father, Creator,
source of all knowledge, wisdom, and skill,
we rejoice in all the gifts
you have bestowed upon us
for the purposes of healing.
We give thanks
for all who work in intensive care,
for their skill and expertise,
and for the equipment they employ.
May they use all these gifts
for the benefit of those in their charge.
Grant them the satisfaction
of success in their endeavours.
Give them serenity
when their efforts are in vain.
Enable them to bring courage and reassurance
to all for whom they care.
In the name of Jesus Christ, our Lord.

THE DYING ▦

A PHONE call from one of the local clergy sent me looking for Gwen. He had told me that she had been admitted for terminal care. What he omitted to tell me—perhaps even he did not know—was that she was actively dying. She was dozing as I approached the bed, but I thought it appropriate to rouse her gently and tell her who I was. Time, I knew, might be short. I discovered that she knew, certainly better than I, probably better than anyone, just how short time was.

She told me that she was dying. She had put all her affairs in order. She had talked with her children, all adult, so that there would be no 'unfinished business' still outstanding after her death.

She had made arrangements for her invalid husband, about whom she was particularly anxious. She had said farewell to the congregation of her local church. She had received the sacraments for the last time and received a final blessing. There was nothing left to be done and nothing for me to do. She could give herself over to death which came quickly and peacefully the next day.

Alison was younger, in her fifties. She had been admitted to Guy's for treatment for her advanced cancer. The treatment had not been successful, confirming her own realistic expectations, and she was preparing to return home to die. She also had put her material affairs in order, but spiritual questions still remained. We talked at length about the basics of the Christian faith: the love of God, forgiveness and acceptance through Jesus Christ, death, resurrection, and eternal life. She was glad to receive the sacraments and derived peace and strength from them. I ministered to her the day before she was due to leave. We said goodbye knowing that we would never again meet in this life, trusting in faith that our next meeting would be in God's nearer presence and beyond time.

However, not all deaths are so peaceful or well managed. Dorothy, a lady of over seventy, was well aware that she was dying, but refused to let go. Her two daughters were with her night and day for a week or more, expecting her death at any time. Their children came in to see their grandmother as and when they were able. Dorothy could find no peace or tranquillity. She was in pain and distress but fought the medication that might have brought her some relief. Finally death took her in a merciful release, but it was a traumatic end to life which both her family and the ward staff found extremely difficult to cope with.

> Lord Jesus Christ,
> Lord of life
> and conqueror of death,
> look in compassion on all
> whose life is drawing to its close.
> As they pass
> through the valley of the shadow of death
> may they know that you are with them.
> May they fear no evil.
> May they give themselves to you
> in trust and faith.
> May they find peace and tranquillity
> in your nearer presence,
> and grant them
> a place in your eternal kingdom,
> now and for ever.
>
> Heavenly Father,
> to your loving care
> we commit all those
> who watch and wait
> with people they know and love.
> Enable them to welcome

the moment of death
as friend, not foe,
knowing that all love in this life
flows from your love,
which is stronger than death itself,
as you have shown us
in the living, dying, and rising
of your Son, Jesus Christ our Lord.

THE DEATH OF A CHILD ▩

ITHIN our own family, all the four grandparents, born around the turn of the century, lost a brother or sister at birth or in infancy. Although the loss for the family was hard to bear, it was never a complete surprise. Conditions were such that parents' expectations for their children had to include the possibility at least that the latter might not survive to maturity.

All that has changed during the intervening years. Great progress has been made in general health, and in the care and treatment of children. Infant mortality has dropped dramatically. The possibility that a child might not survive its illness no longer represents a source of anxiety to most parents.

The death of a child, when it does occur, is therefore all the more devastating. Many young parents have never been faced by death before and least of all expect to meet it for the first time in their own child. 'It isn't right for parents to be burying their children. Children are supposed to bury their parents.' Sadly, it does not always work out that way.

Another concern is what will happen to the dead child. Where will the soul of the child be after death? Who will look after the child and give it the care and affection it knew in this life from its parents? The story in St Mark's Gospel, chapter 10, of Jesus welcoming the children to him is often used to provide a picture of God's love in the life to come, and may be of some help.

However, some siblings have reacted badly to this image and to being told that the dead child has 'gone to Jesus'. For them Jesus becomes an object of resentment and hatred for taking their brother or sister away.

For parents, the dead child can never be replaced. Some couples have another baby almost immediately, others need more time or never have any more children. But however many children parents have or will have, they will always have one more and there will always be a place for that dead child as a member of the family. The feelings of loss may take a long time to fade. As the years go by, especially at anniversaries and festivals, parents will remember their dead child and wonder what he or she would have looked like and grown up to be had death not intervened.

They will also need to be aware of the dangers of transferring the hopes and expectations they had of the dead child on to its surviving brothers and sisters, and any subsequently born. It is all too easy for them to burden their other children with the search for vicarious fulfilment.

> Lamentation is heard in Ramah,
> and bitter weeping:
> Rachel weeping for her children.
> She refuses to be comforted: they are no more.
>
> (Jeremiah 31: 15)

Jesus went to a town called Nain . . . As he approached the gate . . . he met a funeral. The dead man was the only son of his widowed mother . . . When the Lord saw her, his heart went out to her and he said, 'Do not weep'.   (Luke 7: 11–13)

> **Father,**
> **as your Son our Lord Jesus Christ**
> **was touched in his heart**
> **for the widow at Nain,**
> **look in compassion**
> **on all parents who mourn**
> **the loss of their child.**

Help them to see
that their ability to enjoy
the closeness of love
lays them open as well
to sorrow and grief.

May they know above all
that both joy and pain
find their home within you
and within the heart of your son,
Jesus Christ our Lord.

CHILDREN IN HOSPITAL ▣

P EOPLE may remember throughout their lives their
experience in hospital as a child. Children find themselves in
different surroundings with unfamiliar faces, and a buzz
of activity never known before. No wonder, therefore, that most
hospitals nowadays prepare children for admission into hospital,
letting them visit the hospital beforehand and meeting some of the
staff in order to reduce the risk of trauma. A few children even
look forward to their stay, but for most, and for those whose
admission is unpredicted, there may be a level of psychological as
well as physical suffering. A considerable amount of time, effort,
and money is therefore spent on producing a relaxed and happy
atmosphere in a children's ward. The routines and activities of a
child's day in hospital are kept as far as possible like those at home.
Parents are encouraged to live in the hospital or to visit as often as
they can and it is unusual for children not to have someone they
love close by during their stay. Since play and schooling are
essential to a child's development, much attention is given to this,
whilst the cleaners, play leaders, physiotherapists, pharmacists,
chaplains, social workers, nursing and medical staff work towards
creating an atmosphere conducive not only to the child's
well-being, but to the child's family as a whole.

There is an inevitable distinction between the needs of children
undergoing minor surgery or suffering from the usual range of
childhood illnesses, and those who have chronic or even terminal
illness.

Parents of the first group experience the frustrations and
inconvenience of having a child in hospital but know that in a short
time life will return to normal. The second group, however, will
experience a far deeper emotional trauma which, along with the

child's intense suffering, may last for a long time. Hospital life for them will become part of normal life.

Staff in hospital spend a great deal of time meeting the emotional needs of the parents and particularly those with very sick children, while the parents perform many of the routine tasks like bathing and feeding their children. Parents themselves are in a strange environment when they initially come to the hospital and need time to adapt. The longer the child's stay in hospital the greater the pressures, and practical problems such as finding time to keep the home running, holding down a job, and the financial burden of travelling and eating out assume ever greater proportions. If parents have other children at home, they may have to cope with the feelings of jealousy from these children, resentful of the time their parents have to spend away from them. Parents naturally become very stressed and very tired, and need a sympathetic ear and a place of escape.

Staff on paediatric wards also experience pressures peculiar to those working with sick children. It is possible for them to feel swamped by the nature of the work, caring, in many instances, for babies whose only means of communicating pain and discomfort is by crying. Parents' levels of stress and anxiety are often high, and it is particularly difficult for everyone, including other parents, when a child dies. From time to time, difficult moral decisions have to be made and it may not always be easy for staff to maintain a calm and professional detachment from the situation.   (Vera Wootten: Service Manager, Paediatrics)

Jesus said: Let the children come to me . . . for the Kingdom of God belongs to such as these.   (Mark 10: 14)

Lord Jesus Christ
you encouraged children
to approach you and be near to you
for you saw in them
the signs of your kingdom.

Draw near, we pray,
to all children who are ill.
Grant them the gifts of your kingdom
    courage and cheerfulness
      healing and strength.

Support in your love
all parents and families,
and staff who care for them.

In your compassion
look upon
their stress, anxiety, and fear,
and grant them to know
that with the children they love
they are held fast in your presence,
now and always.

THE BIRTH OF A BABY ▨

A FEW months ago, I cradled in my arms our first grandchild, just two days old. It was an emotional moment. Thirty years rolled away, and it did not seem all that long since I had been present at the birth of our daughter, her mother, and had held her in my arms for the first time.

Once again the miracle of creation had been repeated, and I was profoundly thankful that it had been repeated in its perfection. The baby had ten fingers, ten toes. There were none of the defects of which I see so many in hospital. This tiny scrap of humanity, which up till a day or so previously had been securely tucked up inside my daughter, was now on the outside, there for me to hold.

I was held in awe at the wonder of creation, at the beginning of this new life with all its potential. I knew rationally that I was no different from any other new and proud grandfather, that our granddaughter was no different from any other baby. But she had arrived safely and she was ours. The divine activity, the life of the whole cosmos across the ages, seemed to be gathered up and expressed through the birth of this child.

I bring you good news, news of great joy . . .   (Luke 2: 10)

God our Father,
author of eternity,
creator of the highest heaven,
when your Son took our flesh
and was born among us,
the heavens opened and the angels sang.

We now join with them rejoicing in the birth of this child.
We give thanks for his/her safe delivery
and for the beginning of this new life.
We pray that the love which created him/her
may continue to nurture him/her
in home and family.
As he/she grows in stature,
may he/she also grow in grace
and in the knowledge of that love
which you have made known to us
in the person of your son, Jesus Christ our Lord.

THE DEATH OF A BABY ▦

IN spite of hopes and expectations, and perhaps even
assumptions, that all will be well, some babies do not survive.
Some are born prematurely and die despite the best efforts of
the staff in the Special Care Baby Unit. Until a few years ago, there
would have been no hope at all for such babies. The technology
and expertise to which many premature babies now owe their lives
were simply not available.

Some babies are stillborn. Parents have the heart-break of
learning that their child whom they have got to know and love in
the womb has died in the last stages of pregnancy. The mother has
to go through the pains of labour, knowing that she will give birth
to a dead child. The grief which the parents naturally feel can
degenerate into personal or mutual recrimination. They may need
much help and support to see one another's point of view, and
understand each other's feelings.

Other children are born with all kinds of congenital defects, and
need immediate specialized treatment including surgical
intervention. Many make a good recovery. Others, sadly, do not.
The death of a baby leaves a void of loss and grief, and a great
mixture of unresolved feelings. The birth of a baby is an emotional
moment for parents at the best of times. When birth and death
follow closely together, parents are unprepared to cope with
complete reversal of all their hopes and expectations for their new
baby. Instead of enjoying the moment of welcome, they are
plunged into the grief of saying goodbye to the child they hardly
knew.

Simeon blessed them and said to Mary his mother, 'This child is destined to be a sign that will be rejected; and you too will be pierced to the heart.'   (Luke 2: 34–5)

Father,
　　　When his parents came to the Temple
　　　to present the Christ-child to you,
　　　Mary was told
　　　that a sword would pierce her heart.
　　　Look in your mercy on parents
　　　whose joy has been turned to sadness
　　　and who have been pierced through the heart
　　　by the loss of their child.
　　　Enable them to know
　　　that in your sight
　　　nothing that is good
　　　is wasted or in vain.
　　　As they created their child in love
　　　by that same love
　　　may they support each other
　　　in their time of need
　　　and find strength in the knowledge
　　　of your eternal love
　　　made known to us
　　　in Jesus Christ our Lord.

MISCARRIAGE ◼

Sadly not all pregnancies come to term. Many end in miscarriage, some in the early stages of pregnancy, some later.

The Miscarriage Association estimates that between a quarter and one fifth of all medically confirmed pregnancies end in miscarriage, i.e. 160,000–200,000 per annum. This does not take into account miscarriages which take place at an early stage before the pregnancy has been medically confirmed. The final number, therefore, is considerably larger.

All the manifestations of loss and grief are expected on the part of parents when they lose a baby or a child. What is much less obvious is that many experience the same feelings when miscarriage occurs. Parents can experience a real sense of bereavement. They may look for reasons in themselves and in each other as to why the miscarriage occurred. It may be difficult to accept simply as 'one of those things'. In instances where there has been a sequence of miscarriages, and the mother appears to find it difficult to carry babies to term or get beyond a certain stage of her pregnancy, the parents may share a real despair and depression. This may affect their lives and relationship profoundly, and they may need the support and understanding of family, friends, and a pastor whom they may know and trust.

> **Father**
>> **you have created the world**
>> **as an expression of your love,**
>> **and given to women and men**
>> **to join in your act of creation**
>> **as an expression of their mutual love.**

Be with those whose child
   has died in miscarriage,
May they be close to one another
         support one another
         care for one another
         comfort one another
and grow in love and understanding together.

MALFORMED BABIES ✦

ONE afternoon I was called to the Maternity Unit. A young mother had asked to see me before she underwent a termination of pregnancy. Her twenty-week scan had shown that her baby was badly malformed, and after much responsible discussion with her husband, they had decided together that the pregnancy should be terminated.

It was a difficult decision to make, and the mother went to see her local minister. She was not entirely clear why. Perhaps she wanted some sort of blessing, at least some degree of reassurance. Certainly she needed his support. Unfortunately, it was not forthcoming. He told her that she needed to hold firm to her faith and spoke to her of the need for repentance. It took me a long while before I felt I had begun to repair some of the damage which he had inflicted.

Another couple, deeply committed Christians, in a similar situation, decided to bring their malformed child to term. They equally needed to be reassured that they had made the right decision. Their baby was clearly deformed, but even so, her parents found her beautiful, and were thankful for her short life. I baptized her, and helped to prepare the parents to hand her back to God.

> **We acknowledge before you**
> **our perplexity and grief**
> **when our procreation**
> **produces children who,**
> **though made in your image,**
> **suffer malformation.**

We thank you
for their brief lives
for the love which created them
for the love which surrounds them
for the love which they themselves
have created in return.

We pray
for all parents and families
bereaved in this way
of their children,
and of the hopes and expectations
which they held for them.

May they know
that they are sustained
by your complete and perfect love
made known to us in Jesus,
your Son, our Lord.

TERMINATION OF PREGNANCY ▨

T HE telephone rang. A young woman's voice asked me if it would be possible to hold a memorial service for the child of a pregnancy which she had recently had terminated. The child, according to tests, would have been grossly malformed, and would have had no prospect of a normal life. She and her husband had thought long and hard before reaching the decision. Now that the operation had been performed, the parents felt that they should have some form of service to mark the child's brief existence, and the fact that they had willingly but responsibly brought it to an end. We agreed a date, and held a short service.

A year later, the phone rang again. It was the same mother. Could we hold another short memorial service for her aborted daughter, on the anniversary of her death, this time naming her, something which she, the mother, had omitted to do last time. Again I met the family and held a short memorial service. As before, they brought a posy and lit a candle in the chapel.

A year later, another phone call. Could we mark the second anniversary especially important now as the mother was pregnant again, soon to be delivered, and needed to 'lay to rest' the terminated child before the new baby was born. Again, we held a short service, naming the dead child before God. It was obvious that no matter how many children there would eventually be in the family, there would always be an extra one. The terminated child would always have its place.

You it was who fashioned
my inward parts;
you knitted me together
in my mother's womb.
My body was no mystery to you,
when I was formed in secret,
woven in the depths of the earth.

Your eyes foresaw my deeds,
and they were all recorded
in your book;
my life was fashioned
before it had come into being

(Psalm 139: 13, 15, 16)

Father
We pray for parents who,
    responsibly
    painfully
    and after much thought
have decided to terminate
    the life of the child
    which they have created.
Enable them to live with their decision
and may their child continue to live
    in their hearts and minds
    as a member of their family,
    and of your eternal family,
    now and for ever.

MEDICAL RESEARCH ◈

FROM time to time there are stories in the news telling us that there has been a 'breakthrough'. Another significant step has been made in the understanding, diagnosis, and treatment of some particular disease.

Behind that announcement lie long periods of painstaking and often tedious research. The process and results are carefully detailed and verified. What cannot be quantified, however, is the amount of human insight, inspiration, ingenuity, and sheer dogged perseverance. It can be difficult for a researcher to know where a programme of work is leading. The results may not be what was expected or, indeed, there may be no results at all. A decision has to be made as to whether the research programme should continue, be discontinued, or switched in a different direction.

A further and deeper question exists: how are advances in medical knowledge to be used? Or will they be abused? Pure science is not matched by human frailty, greed, and cynicism, and may find itself seduced for base ends and ulterior motives.

In spite of these dangers people engaged on medical research need to remain open to perceive the marvellous intricacy of the secrets which they are uncovering and bringing to the store of human knowledge. In religious terms, they are brought face to face with the wonder of God's creation. In human terms, they are faced with the need for humility as they confront the delicate balance built into the structure of our universe.

When I look up at your heavens,
   the work of your fingers,
at the moon and the stars you
   have set in place,
what is a frail mortal, that
   you should be mindful of him,
a human being, that you should
   take notice of him?

(Psalm 8: 3–4)

O Lord our God, the source of all truth and the goal of all
knowledge; we thank you for the achievements of medical
science. We pray for those engaged in study and research. Give
them wisdom and imagination in their investigations and
compassion and patience in their dealings with others. Grant
them reverence for both life and truth, so that the lives of many
may be enriched; through Jesus Christ our Lord.
(The London Committee of Licensed Teachers of Anatomy of the London
Medical Schools: an ecumenical service of thanksgiving)

ORGAN TRANSPLANTATION ◈

ONE of the most painful memories I have is being called late one afternoon to the Children's Intensive Care Unit. A little girl had been brought in and died very suddenly. The parents had decided that her organs should be donated for transplantation. I arrived on the ward about an hour before the child was due to go to theatre. Her mother and father wanted me to say a blessing as part of their farewell and letting go. She was a lovely child with long fair hair, totally unmarked by accident or illness. She appeared to be just sleeping, and it was difficult to believe that she had been diagnosed as brain dead. I did as the parents asked of me, spent a little time with them, and left them alone.

The next morning there was a message on my answer-phone from the vicar of a parish in another part of the country. A boy who was a member of his congregation had been called to Guy's for a transplant. Would I please make contact with him, and minister both to him and his parents as appropriate. It was not too difficult for me to guess where the transplanted organ had come from, and it gave me a strange sort of feeling as the bearer of this knowledge. It was made sadder when, a few weeks later, the transplant was rejected, and had to be removed.

A happier outcome of transplant surgery was experienced by the man whose new kidney worked successfully. As I arrived to give him Holy Communion he asked that we should include a special prayer of thanksgiving not only for himself but for the generosity of the unknown donor and their family. We prayed that in their loss they might be comforted, knowing that some good had come out of the tragedy which had befallen them, and that the loss of their loved one had not been totally in vain.

Heavenly Father,
who through your Son
brought life out of death;
we thank you for those who,
engulfed by the sudden death of their loved ones,
have seen the vision of hope
for others in need.
We give thanks for the skill and expertise
of those who perform transplant surgery,
and of those who care
for transplanted patients.
Prosper their work with good success,
and may those who have received
the gift of new organs
use their new life for the benefit of all
in the light of your goodness towards us.

AIDS ▨

AIDS is the fastest growing disease of our time. Estimates vary as to how many people will be affected by the turn of the century but by any reckoning, the numbers are vast. The disease, which is thought to have originated among male homosexuals, is now widely spread through the heterosexual population, especially in India and Africa. People affected there are amongst the poorest and those least able to cope with the disease or prevent its spread. Increasingly, babies are being born with AIDS, and thus the disease is being passed on to the innocent sufferers of a second generation.

There are those within the churches who would claim that this is ample evidence of the wrath of God, and his punishment of moral evil-doers. It is presented as a classic example of the sins of the fathers being visited on their children at least to the second, if not succeeding generations. Passages from both the Old Testament and the New are quoted to support this view. However, other voices would claim that no matter how the disease was contracted, it is the duty of the Christian Church to show compassion, and do whatever it can to support AIDS patients and their families in order to relieve their distress, social and emotional as well as physical.

There is much painful discussion about what the Church's attitudes to AIDS should be. Around this debate cluster other issues such as the Church's attitude towards homosexuality and towards sexual relationships in general. The Churches have to find how best to follow and apply the example of Jesus, who came not to be served but to serve, and to share the common life of his people in the circumstances in which he found them.

Loving God
warm our hearts with the fire of your spirit and help us
    to accept the challenge of HIV and AIDS.
Protect the healthy, calm the frightened, give courage to
    those in pain, comfort the dying,
and keep the departed in your unending love.
May we your people,
with energy and imagination,
and trust in your steadfast love,
be united with one another
to conquer all disease, fear, and prejudice.
We make this prayer
confident in your mercy and compassion
now and for ever.

ALCOHOLISM ▩

'Y OU'RE a vicar. You're shupposhed to know all about these things.' He was an alcoholic. He was full of drink. His wife was desperately ill in the intensive care unit. And he was very angry. The sight of a priest made his anger even worse, and he vented its full force on me. The abuse very quickly became personal, and what I hoped was my cool, reasoned approach gave way to anger. I knew I had handled the situation badly, and that upset me. But I was also upset for the man's family, who sat by in embarrassed silence, and for the man himself. At a time when his wife needed him and the support of his presence, his addiction had taken him over. He was no use to her or to anyone else, and my confrontation with him had only made matters worse.

Despite my own personal feeling about this episode there is a generally lenient attitude towards drunkenness and even alcoholism. Alcohol is easily available, and is regarded as a social lubricant. It is, in fact, a depressant rather than a stimulant, and achieves its effect by lowering people's inhibitions. People who have had too much to drink are often called 'merry', and regarded as a source of amusement. On the other hand, alcohol abuse can cause untold misery and suffering in terms of broken lives and broken homes. It has been estimated that deaths caused by, or related to alcohol may be the third most common category in the UK after heart disease and cancer in its various forms.

Alcoholism is difficult to treat. Many alcoholics are reluctant or unwilling to acknowledge their dependence on alcohol, or having acknowledged it, to give it up. Those who look after them, both at home and in hospital, need enormous resources of emotional strength and stamina, understanding and resilience, to cope with all the demands made upon them.

Lord, out of the depths I have called to you.

(Psalm 130. 1)

———

Father
we confess our misuse
of the good things
you have given to us,
through weakness and irresponsibility,
through selfish pleasure and over-indulgence.

Look in your mercy on those
who are addicted and dependent,
and who damage the lives of others
by the ruin of their own.

May they be able to discern
the light of Christ
in the darkness which surrounds them,
and grasp the meaning of his Resurrection,
that the chains of despair and death are broken,
and that out of the depths
there rises the promise of life renewed.

Father
we pray for all who work
with those who are addicts.
Give them wisdom and patience,
and the ability to perceive
the true needs of those
who come to them for help.
Grant them to know
that as they minister
the healing love of Jesus,
they are themselves sustained by him
who knew the needs of all mankind.

DRUG ADDICTION

As I was thinking about writing this section, two events coincided. When I came home in the evening, the local free newspaper lay on the doormat. I picked it up and read the headline, 'New lifeline for crack addicts'. The report went on to quote a Drugline counsellor: 'Drugs have become very prevalent in this part of the world. If you go down to any of the estates with £25 in your pocket you'll be able to buy some. Addicts can go through absolute hell. Unlike heroin addicts who can get methadone, there is no medication for crack or cocaine. They can spend hundreds of pounds, and do more and more desperate things to get it.'

The next morning, I had an unusual telephone call. A young man rang to ask me if I would go with him to the mortuary to see the body of his girlfriend. She had been murdered the night before, and had been brought into Guy's. It was a grim sight. She had obviously been badly beaten before being stabbed. Her background, I was told, was one of drugs, crime, and prostitution stretching back over many years. The whole grim story of drug addiction was summed up in that tragic body laid out for us to see in the mortuary chapel.

If I climb up to heaven, you are there; if I make my bed in Sheol, you are there. (Psalm 139: 8)

He descended to the dead. (The Apostles' Creed)

Lord Jesus,
after your death upon the cross
you descended to the dead
yet rose to new life
on the third day.

Be with all those
who experience the hell
of drug addiction.

Be near to them
in their personal darkness.
Give them the will to break free
from the habit which chains
and enslaves them.
Enable them to taste the freedom
of life renewed.

Be with all those
who work with them and for them.
Sustain them at times
of disappointment and danger
and prosper their efforts
with good success.
We ask this
for your name's sake.

MENTAL ILLNESS ◈

S PEAKING at the launch of a national schizophrenia
research appeal in May 1991, the Prince of Wales said
that mental illness was one of the most intractable
taboos remaining in society. He developed his theme in terms
of the wide-reaching effect of mental illness on the community
and the extra resources needed to deal with it. He did not,
apparently, venture any suggestions as to why the taboo should
exist.

The reason, in fact, is not hard to find. It is estimated that one
person in five of the population in the United Kingdom will require
treatment for mental illness at some stage of their lives. The
possibility of mental illness therefore poses a significant threat to
us all.

Sometimes the threat is mistakenly interpreted or anticipated.
There may be occasions when people feel they are 'going mad'
because of the depths of sheer human misery and unhappiness
which accompany times of stress or the breakdown of personal
relationships. They may therefore consult their GP about their
feelings of depression, and receive medication to help tide them
over the crisis in their life and life-style.

In other instances there can be no doubt regarding the
pathological nature of the mental disturbance. People may be
deeply withdrawn into depression or suffering the more florid
symptoms of schizophrenia. They may hear voices which
persecute them and encourage them to destroy themselves.

For some, the religious element in their delusion may be strong.
I remember one young man who told me that he was Jesus, the
Blessed Virgin Mary was his mother, and the Pope was his father.
He had just received a message from them that he should ask me

to exorcize him. Other people may suffer from long-standing personality disorders which may disrupt both their own lives and the lives of those who look after them.

Mental illness is very real but very different from physical illness, and for this reason still carries the stigma and therefore the taboo referred to by the Prince of Wales. Physical illness is usually susceptible to medical and/or surgical intervention. Mental illness is far less clear-cut, far less tangible, far less predictable.

There is less certainty about its treatment and the outcome of treatment. What is certain is that mental illness is extremely difficult to live with, both for the patients and for their families. Yet mental illness does not command the immediate emotive appeal which is extended to people, say, who have undergone transplant surgery or who are terminally ill. This is reflected in the amount of resources and support which mental illness attracts—or fails to attract—nationally.

There seems to lurk still the suspicion that if only people would 'pull themselves together and snap out of it', there would be nothing wrong with them. Perhaps that is the ultimate form of treating mental illness as an 'intractable taboo'.

> If I make my bed in Sheol,
>   you are there
>
> .   .   .   .
>
> If I say 'Surely darkness will steal over me,
>   and the day around me turn to night',
> darkness is not too dark for you
> and night is as light as day;
> to you both dark and light are one.
>
> (Psalm 139: 8, 11–12)

When they came to Jesus and saw the madman . . . sitting there clothed and in his right mind, they were afraid.   (Mark 5: 15)

Lord Jesus Christ,
you healed those who suffered
in mind as well as body.
Look in your compassion
on people among us who are mentally ill.

We pray for all
   who are driven by depression to the depths of despair
   who attempt to end their own lives
   who are victims of obsession
   who are persecuted by the voices they hear
   who live in a world of their own
   who are violent or withdrawn
   who are plagued by religious delusions.

Take from them all unreality.
Help them to know that in the depths
   you search for them
and that in your presence
   you hold them secure.
Grant to them wholeness of mind
so that they may be at peace,
at one with themselves
and at one with you.
We ask this for your name's sake.

PEOPLE WITH SPECIAL LEARNING DIFFICULTIES ▧

EMMALINE is one of the people I shall always remember. She was already in her early nineties when I knew her, a bright and chirpy person whose whole outlook and personality belied her age. Yet Emmaline had spent most of her long life within the confines of a large hospital for mentally handicapped people. In the days when Emmaline arrived there, before the First World War, the label was even worse: they were mentally subnormal or mental defectives.

The reasons for Emmaline being there were lost in the mists of time, although her records must have existed. Perhaps they showed that she had committed some minor misdemeanour. To have an illegitimate child or to be convicted of petty theft were sufficient in themselves to earn the condemnation of being 'morally deficient', and therefore of being committed to a long-stay institution.

Fortunately, Emmaline had survived the institution. Even better, she had learned how to use the system to her own advantage. Nevertheless, she realized with regret how circumscribed her life had been, and that life offered far more than she had ever been able to enjoy. The last news I heard of her was that she was being discharged from hospital to live in the community for her last few years.

There are those, however, who will continue to need the support and care of a long-stay hospital. Their degree of learning difficulties prevents them from leading a normal life in the community, and they would not be able to fend for themselves. Sometimes, also, people suffer from physical as well as learning difficulties. Whatever may be their disability, it is important to remember that people are people, each with their own personality and characteristics. We attach labels to each other and pigeon-hole one another far too easily. At last we are becoming aware of this and realize the hurt and offence that the stigma of being categorized in certain ways may cause. Whoever we are, we need to treat each other with the dignity which is due to people created in the image of God.

_____

God created human beings in his own image;
in the image of God he created them.

(Genesis 1: 27)

_____

Heavenly Father,
you care for all that you have created,
for all your people are made in your own image.

Surround with your love
all who experience difficulties in daily living
caused through defects before birth,
or accidents during life.
We thank you
for their gifts of spontaneity and affection,
and for all that they can bring
to enrich the lives of others.
May they reach out to you
with unfettered love,
and know you as Father
and Jesus as their friend
in the fellowship of your Spirit.

'IN THE COMMUNITY' ▣

ECENT years have seen the run-down and closure of many of the hospitals caring for people suffering from psychiatric disorders and learning difficulties. Many of these hospitals were large. Most of them were old. Inevitably they represented some of the worst features of institutionalization amongst staff and patients alike. On the positive side, however, patients were looked after with real care and much affection, and many lived out their days in such hospitals. For them, over the years, the hospital became their home. While on one hand, it deprived them of independence, on the other it provided them with shelter, safety, and security. The hospital offered asylum, in the real sense.

Many of the people who are discharged from the long-stay hospitals to live 'in the community' miss the feeling of security which the institution, for all its faults, had offered them. They have to take on the responsibilities of daily living which many of them feel ill-equipped to deal with. They may also discover that the 'community' into which they have been discharged is either unwelcoming or at worst positively hostile. Hospital staff, planning for the discharge of patients into the community, often work hard to bridge the gap, but with varying degrees of success. Old attitudes die hard. The reasons why most of the old long-stay institutions were built out of town, sometimes out of sight, and behind high walls, still persist.

It is easy to talk about 'the community', but it is an entity which is often difficult to perceive. This is especially true of the large conurbations where, unfortunately, most former patients find themselves. Even where 'the community' is more discernible, and the community spirit can be felt, it is by no means certain that this will be extended to include people who have spent so long in hospital. We can be slow to accept people who show themselves to be different, sometimes in rather bizarre ways, from ourselves whom we perceive as normal.

Of the taboos of life, sex has been dealt with. Death is currently holding our attention. Learning difficulties pose no threat but we are distinctly uneasy with mental illness. Our reluctance to commit ourselves to becoming a cohesive community, which cares for people on its margins, tells us a great deal about ourselves.

> **Father of all,**
> **we lay before you**
> **our plans for care in the community.**
> **Our intention is**
> **fellowship and welcome,**
> **caring and hope for the future;**
> **but we acknowledge with penitence**
> **that too often the words convey**
> **harshness and lack of sympathy,**
> **isolation and unfriendliness.**
>
> **We pray for all**
> **who have been discharged from hospital**
> **to live in the community.**
> **Enable them to cope**
> **with the realities of life,**
> **perplexity and insecurity,**
> **and enable us all**
> **to learn from them**
> **for they have much to teach us**
> **in your name.**

Father,
we pray for all who provide and promote
care in the community.
Enable them to use
their skill and experience,
wisdom and imagination,
so that those who are discharged from hospital
may find wholeness and fulfilment
in their new life,
and grow as people into your image
which you have shown us
in Jesus, your Son, our Lord.

CARE OF THE ELDERLY ▣

'I NEVER thought I should end up like this', said Rose. She was in her eighties, more or less blind, but still acutely aware of herself and of her situation. It had not been long since her previous hospital admission which had lasted several weeks. When she had been discharged, she had gone to stay with her daughter, and then, when she was well enough, she had returned to her own flat. But she had had a fall, fortunately not a bad one, nor had she been lying too long before help arrived. However, back she came to hospital, visibly less well and weaker than the time before, also it seemed, more tired and perhaps a little perplexed, trying to make sense of the situation in relation to herself and her own feelings. Within herself she felt the same Rose that she had always been, yet she knew that her body was failing and was no longer able to respond in the way that it had in the past. She wished it would continue to respond but recognized that her years were against her. Knowing Rose a little, I guessed that a time might come soon when the effort of going on living would become too much for her, and, weary of life, she would choose, like so many old people, to give up the struggle and depart peacefully.

Rose was a faithful member of her local church and she received Holy Communion regularly in hospital. This seemed enough for her. She did not want to take our conversation in the direction of thinking about life and death, and what might be beyond. A few elderly people want to talk about these things. The majority, like Rose, appear not to want to do so. It is quite impossible to generalize, and even worse to impose one's own expectations.

It is also impossible to generalize about what constitutes an 'old' person. Some people are old at fifty, like the man who told me he did not want promotion because he was unwilling to take on extra responsibilities 'at his age'. By contrast, an old man of ninety-four, who had spent all his life working his smallholding in the fens, told me that he had just invested in a new rotovator. People carry their personality traits and characteristics with them into old age. They are not necessarily sweet and gentle because they are elderly, neither are they aggressive and cantankerous. What they can offer us is an added perspective on life as we know it, viewed from the experience of years, neither better, nor worse, but seen differently with the passage of time. This dimension is both valuable and necessary. Perhaps the worst disservice we can render the elderly is to make them feel value-less because of the attitudes and expectations we place upon them.

> Lord Jesus,
> you taught us that what we do
> for the least of all your children
> we do also for you.
>
> Be with all whose work
> is caring for elderly people.
> Grant to them a genuine interest
> for those in their care.
> Enable them to see them as
> people with needs
> > history
> > achievements
> > personality.
> Help them to maintain
> the independence of thought,
> choice, and action
> of those in their care.
> And in your good time
> enable them to help those who are dying
> to a peaceful end.

Be with all those who are ripe in age.
Help them to know that as you have guided them
and been their companion over the years,
so you will travel with them to the end.
As bodily strength declines
may their faith in you grow stronger
so that without fear but with confidence
in your unfailing presence
they may offer themselves to you,
and find rest and peace at the last
in your eternal love.

II

SITUATIONS IN HOSPITAL CARE

VICTIMS OF CIRCUMSTANCE ◈

JIM was complaining bitterly and, it seemed, with some justification. Nothing had gone right for him over the last few years. He had lost his job and had been involved in an accident which left him with a disability. He had been out of work for some years during which he had suffered a mental breakdown. He had stayed at home and looked after his invalid mother without much family support, and virtually none from the statutory services. She had been diagnosed as suffering from cancer but there were administrative hold-ups which delayed her being transferred to a hospice. She deteriorated and died very quickly before she could be admitted there. Jim could not be contacted, and he came to the hospital not knowing that his mother had died. When he was told, he was understandably bitter and wept copiously. At every stage, the system had failed him. He seemed to have fallen through the net at every turn and, through no fault of his own, to be one of life's losers. He was angry and frustrated, very much the victim of circumstance.

> **Lord Jesus Christ,**
> **as you handed yourself over**
> **to the events of your passion,**
> **you experienced powerlessness**
> **and the bitter pains of death.**
>
> **Be with all those**
> **who are overwhelmed by the events of life,**
> **who are rendered powerless by them,**
> **and feel bitterness, anger, and resentment.**

Grant them to know
that as they walk with you now
the way of the cross,
so you will lead them
beyond death to resurrection
where they may find
new life in you,
and peace and fulfilment
within themselves
according to your promises.

Almighty Father
Look with mercy on this your family
for which our Lord Jesus Christ
  was content to be betrayed
  and given up into the hands of wicked men
  and to suffer death upon the cross;
  who is alive and glorified
  with you and the Holy Spirit,
  one God, now and for ever.

> (*The Alternative Service Book 1980*, Collect for
> Good Friday)

ACCIDENTS ◈

ONE of the useful functions of radio, whether national or local, is to provide up-to-the-moment traffic news. There are warnings of delays, diversions, and hold-ups. Often these are caused by accidents. But I sometimes wonder whether these so-called accidents really are accidents. I believe it is fair to ask, when is an accident not an accident?

'Accident' is derived from the Latin word meaning 'to happen'. Thus, an accident is basically 'a happening', an unforeseen event which occurs by chance. So I may slip on a wet pavement and twist my ankle. No one is at fault. It is simply 'one of those things'—an accident. However, if I slipped because my shoes were worn and were not likely to give me a grip on the wet pavement, and I had neglected to get them mended, that can hardly be an accident. It was always a possibility that I might slip and the responsibility was mine. If, however, I was walking along on a dry day and caught my foot on a loose or uneven paving stone, is this simply an accident, or the result of bad workmanship, and therefore negligence on someone's part?

Similarly, it seems difficult to speak of 'accidents' when a hundred or more vehicles are involved in a series of pile-ups in fog on one of the motorways and several people are killed. Equally, I find it difficult to believe that it really was 'an accident' when two vehicles crashed head-on on a straight road otherwise deserted, on a bright summer afternoon, leaving two people dead and another, now a widow, seriously injured in hospital. On the other hand, I can regard it as an accident when a two-year-old boy darted through a door, left open only for a few seconds, and ran out into the path of an oncoming car.

It is easy to be glib with the word 'accident', to use it as a convenient coverall which hides, by its over-use and familiarity, the pain and trauma of the people involved, and the shock experienced by their families and friends. We want the accident cleared out of the way as quickly as possible so that we can get on with our journey and reach our destination. The least we can do is to hold in prayer for a moment or two the people who have been involved.

> Merciful Father,
> we bring to you
> all who have been involved in accidents,
> unforeseen chances,
> or events which arise
> from the responsibility of others.
>
> Enable them to cope
> with the pain of their injuries,
> and the shock of their experience.
> Be with their families and friends
> in the turmoil of their feelings.
> In the knowledge of your presence
> may they find healing and peace.

Be present, O merciful God, in all time of our need, so that we who are wearied by the changes and chances of this mortal world may rest upon your eternal changelessness.   (Adapted from the Office of Compline)

WHY, LORD? ◼

THOSE words are repeated, either knowingly or unknowingly, by many people who find themselves in trouble. The words frame a natural response to death and a variety of losses which cause feelings of shock, horror, and disbelief, or even no feelings at all—a state of complete and utter numbness. They are a 'natural response' because they convey anger and protest at the unfairness of circumstances. Where is the justice of innocent suffering? What can anyone have done to deserve such apparent punishment? The protest is often condensed into a simple word: why?

There is little use in pointing out that life is not based on a system of rewards and punishments. It simply does not work that way. Nor is there any credibility in the old, trite saying, 'these things are sent to try us'. Who sends them—and why? And if, therefore, all this has anything to do with God, what kind of God is he and why should he choose to inflict such suffering on his people whom he professes to love? If he is 'almighty' and 'Father', as so many of our prayers begin, why is it that he is apparently incapable of preventing pain and suffering or, at least, chooses not to?

At this point we are dealing with the great mysteries of life and death. People are trying to make sense of circumstances which apparently defy any meaning. There are no easy answers at all. There are, however, two possible clues.

The first is that to suffer pain is part of our humanity. We are sensitive creatures, able to appreciate art, music, beauty, honesty, goodness, the love and acceptance of people around us. But such sensitivity lays us open to pain of all kinds, from toothache to heartache, to the pain of loss and deprivation of what we value most.

The second clue is to be found in the fact that God enters into and shares our human condition in Jesus. Jesus knew in his short life a whole range of human experience and emotion: joy, happiness, and personal fulfilment as well as sorrow, anger, disappointment, apparent failure, and rejection. As he hung on the cross, there came to his lips the words of the psalm, and he cried aloud, 'My God, my God, why have you forsaken me?' Jesus made those words his own. He united for all time the suffering of humankind with the heart of God. Wherever there is pain and anguish, God is already there.

For I am convinced that there is nothing in death or life . . . nothing in all creation that can separate us from the love of God in Christ Jesus our Lord.   (Romans 8: 38, 39)

My God, my God, why have you forsaken me?

(Psalm 22: 1)

Lord Jesus,
you hung upon the cross,
and cried out to the Father
in the pain of desolation
and the agony of dereliction.
Look now in your mercy
upon all whose suffering
is without comprehension
or meaning or purpose,
and who cry to you
in their distress.

Make known to them
that no suffering is beyond you,
no pain beyond your understanding,
and that wherever they are
you have been there before.

By the compassion of your humanity,
take away the isolation
and loneliness of their pain;
may they find oneness and peace
with you and with the Father
within the heart and the Spirit
of the suffering God.

THE SEARCH FOR MEANING ▣

> When I look up at your heavens
>> the work of your fingers,
> at the moon and the stars
>> you have set in place,
> what is a frail mortal,
>> that you should be mindful of him,
> a human being, that you should
>> take notice of him?
>
> (Psalm 8: 3–4)

So wrote the psalmist some 3,000 years ago. His words have passed into the Judaeo-Christian tradition, and become part of a rich storehouse of spirituality and inspiration. The psalmist was contemplating the world around him, the majesty and beauty of creation, pondering the place of mankind within it, and searching for meaning and purpose in life as he knew it.

The experience of being in hospital, or having a loved one in hospital, can create a search for meaning. People need to make sense of what is happening to them. They find themselves grappling with a range of ideas, thoughts, and feelings which may be quite new to them and which they now find very difficult to cope with; they are easily reduced to a series of clichés by which they seek to express their perplexity and their consciousness of the vastness of the problems confronting them.

Take Maggie, for instance, in hospital for an extended course of treatment. She was a rough sort of person and made no pretence at refinement or culture. Her language was colourful and unrestrained no matter to whom she was talking. Thus she made sense of her illness in familiar terms:

You can always see someone worse off than yourself
These things are sent to try us
When your time's up, you've got to go.

More religiously, possibly for my benefit, she added: 'It's all in God's hands.'

Others, bereaved and stunned by sudden death, might have added, 'God always takes the best first.' Or they might pose the question as to why, when there are so many bad people about whose death would be no loss to the world, God should take their loved one who had never done anyone any harm.

It is easy to dismiss such remarks as 'folk religion' and to be condescending about them. On the contrary. We should regard these well-worn sayings as genuine attempts to make sense of difficult and perplexing situations which appear to contradict all the accepted patterns of justice and fairness, reward and punishment, which we like to believe should form the basis of our lives.

We constantly search for meaning, and strive to correlate life as we know it with traditional and accepted Christian teaching about a loving and compassionate God. The search dates back at least to the psalmist, and beyond him is lost in the mists of time.

If we love only through what is good, then it is not God we are loving but something earthly to which we give that name . . . We must love God through the evil that occurs, solely because everything that actually occurs is real and behind all reality stands God.   (Simone Weil)

Knowledge so wonderful is beyond my grasp;
it is so lofty I cannot reach it.

(Psalm 139: 6)

Lord God our Creator,
we stand in awe
before the world
in which we live.
We wonder at its intricacy
                    its complexity
                    its balance
as more and more of its secrets
are revealed by the skill and science
you have given us.

We ponder the meaning of your world
as violence, suffering and pain abound,
and we seek to understand their place
within your plan and purpose
for us and for all your people.

Help us to know
that Jesus your Son
was made one with us,
shared our human life,
and opened wide
his arms upon the cross
to embrace us all.

By his compassion
may our needs be met
        our pain relieved,
and our faith renewed
so that we may know
that life is greater than death,
and that your love is over all.

ANGER ▣

I HAVE met many angry people in hospital. Charlotte was the angriest of them all. She was a small determined woman in her forties, and a regular but not uncritical member of her local church. People's needs were her work and her life. She brought to their welfare the insights and the dynamism of her own personality. She understood people, and knew what made them tick. She knew herself equally well.

She had been treated for cancer a couple of years before I met her, and the treatment had at first been successful. But her cancer had returned, and she underwent radical surgery which affected her bodily functions. Charlotte was devastated, not only physically but emotionally. Every movement of her body was extremely painful and difficult. She felt deep humiliation, disgust, and self-loathing. She wept long and copiously. There was very little one could do to comfort her, even less that one could say. All I could do was to be with her, let her be angry, and not be put off by her anger. Because of her background, she knew what she was doing, and what I was doing. Eventually the eruption of anger would pass, at least temporarily. She would dry her tears, clasp my hand, and thank me for listening. It was enough. She understood, and I understood. There was no need for anything more.

Father
we pray for all whose illness
sets loose within them
bitterness and frustration,
anger and resentment
   against themselves,
   against those who care for them,
   against the world,
   against their loved ones,
   against you.

Help them to be aware
that whatever their feelings,
they are acceptable to you,
and that nothing
can remove them from your presence
or hide them from your sight.

GUILT ▨

WHEN someone dies, a feeling of guilt is commonly experienced by those who are left behind. Sometimes the guilt is real. Conflicts and rifts may be left unresolved because of the intervention of death. Hurtful words may have been spoken for which apologies needed to be expressed. Harmful actions may have been performed for which there should have been atonement. The opportunity for reconciliation is lost for ever.

More commonly, guilt is self-imposed. People feel that they could and should have done more for the dead person, and that they have consequently failed. This feeling may be especially prevalent where accidents have occurred. People blame themselves for having set in motion, all unwittingly, the train of events which culminated in the tragedy. 'If only I'd said I was sorry . . . if only I hadn't shouted at him . . . if only I hadn't bought her the bike . . . taught her how to use it . . . if only he had gone to see the doctor earlier . . . if only she had heeded the warning . . .'

Recriminations abound, towards oneself and towards others. 'I feel hollow inside,' a bereaved relative said to me. Into that hollow creeps the cancer of guilt which makes the grief at parting with a loved one, and the feelings of loss, even harder to bear.

There is another kind of guilt, misplaced but none the less real. Joan had been in hospital for a long time undergoing an extended course of treatment for cancer. A number of patients whom she had known had died on the ward while she had been there. It had given her a 'funny kind of feeling'. 'Why them and not me?' she asked. Her husband told her not to be like that, and to think more positively, but she was experiencing in a real way the 'guilt of the survivor'.

Two babies lay in adjacent cots in the intensive care unit. Both were desperately ill. The parents got to know each other, and supported one another in moments of crisis and stress. Eventually, one of the children died while the other went on to make a full recovery. The parents of the surviving child were badly upset when the other died. Apart from being genuinely concerned for the other parents in their loss, they experienced a considerable degree of guilt because they were thankful that their own child had survived.

At that time the cock crowed for the second time, and Peter remembered how Jesus had said to him; 'Before the cock crows twice, you will disown me three times.' And he burst into tears.   (Mark 14: 72)

> Bringing all my burdens,
>   Sorrow, sin, and care,
> At thy feet I lay them,
>   And I leave them there.
>
>   (Bishop Walsham How, *Hymns*
>   *A and M Revised*)

Come to me, all who are weary and whose load is heavy; I will give you rest.   (Matthew 11: 28)

Most merciful Father,
we bring to you
our burden of guilt,
both real and imagined.
We pray for those
who are crushed by its weight,
especially as they grieve for the loss
of those whom they loved.

May they discover
the Good News of Jesus,
accept for themselves
the saving grace
of his dying and rising,
and through his love
find forgiveness, reconciliation,
and lasting peace.

PAIN ▦

KEN had been under the care of Guy's for about three years. He had had an operation for cancer which had gone well. His prognosis was good, and subsequent tests showed no sign that the disease had spread.

However, he was never free from pain, chronic, debilitating. Despite the best efforts of the experts in that field, there was no relief. Ken became desperate. He even considered getting rid of the pain by ending his life. His pain was completely dominating him, and his family too. Everything they planned, hoped for, achieved, or failed to achieve, was dependent on Ken's level of pain. He and his wife were regular members of their local church, and together they prayed about his condition. 'My faith has been a great support to me,' he said, 'and I couldn't have managed without it. But in the end you start doubting even that, and you wonder whether there is anyone up there.' The hospital staff got to know Ken well and we were all sympathetic. In a sense, we were being drawn into this vortex of pain, and suffered the pain of our own inadequacy because no one seemed able to come up with any solution.

Rosina was completely different. She too suffered from intractable pain and she too was a pillar of her local church. But she came from a different background. She had been brought up to regard pain as something to be suffered for the Lord, in union with him, as part of his own pain and suffering on the cross. Therefore pain was a gift from God, and to suffer pain was a privilege which he reserved for his chosen ones. Rosina was extremely reluctant to accept analgesics, and regarded taking pain-killing tablets as an admission of failure. We tussled with this theological problem in the friendliest kind of way as a matter of pastoral concern. I wanted her to see that medication was a gift from God, and had been discovered and formulated by people using gifts and skills given by God. I also wanted her to share my belief that God's gifts are there for the benefit of his people, and that he does not want any of us to suffer. There was, therefore, no merit in experiencing pain unnecessarily. Rosina remained unconvinced, and was obviously happier to stay with her own point of view, despite the physical discomfort it entailed. We continued our discussions, but had not got further than agreeing to disagree by the time she went home.

———

Lord, out of the depths I have called to you; hear my cry, Lord; let your ears be attentive to my supplication. (Psalm 130: 1, 2)

———

Lord Jesus,
as you were nailed to the cross,
and hung on Calvary,
you experienced
pain and suffering in your body,
and deep anguish within.

Be present, we pray, with all
who through illness or injury
face the suffering of pain
which fills their body,
and overwhelms their being,
causing great weariness,
and undermining their will to live.

When they cry to you
from their personal depths,
grant them to know
that their prayer is heard
and though the pain may not pass,
you are in it too,
and share it with them.
For all pain is yours,

and you pass through it
to resurrection and new life,
and are a constant companion
to all who would follow.

Be with all those
who are caught up
in the pain of the person they love.
Bear them in their feelings
of inadequacy and uselessness,
of frustration and hopelessness,
of resentment and the guilt which follows.
Grant them to know
that in their human
frailty and vulnerability,
they are loved and accepted by you,
for you share our life,
with all its joys and sorrows,
and you died and rose again for us,
and are with us,
now and always.

LOSING CONTROL ❖

A FRIEND of mine was admitted to hospital for an operation—not life-threatening but not exactly routine—one which 'needed doing'. It was one of those situations where the case had involved three different specialities which needed to liaise with each other in order for the operation to be carried out.

It soon became apparent that the liaison left a lot to be desired. After a tiring and trying day in the hospital, stretching from 10 o'clock in the morning until well after 10 in the evening, he was eventually sent home into the care of his GP. Apart from being angry and upset by the obvious inefficiency of the situation, what disturbed him was that he felt out of control. He was being passed from one department to another, yet no one seemed able or willing to make any decisions for his benefit. Nor was he in a position to do so himself.

This was a very minor example, although, I suppose, probably typical of many happening each day. More significant are instances where medical skill and 'know-how' seem to gather a momentum of their own, and desperate attempts are made to save the life of a patient even beyond what a family may reasonably expect and hope for, sometimes to their own cost. They also feel that they are out of control.

Similarly, I have been with many parents at the side of the cot where their child is surrounded by, and linked up to, a massive array of machinery and monitors, tubes, drips, and wires. It is physically impossible for them to do the thing they most want, which is to hold their child. They have handed the child over and they are now effectively out of control.

At the other end of life, old people in hospital may also feel out of control—of their body, their movements, their future. Other people may be taking decisions for them regarding their home, their finances, their pet, their way of life. Control is important to all of us and is something we have developed over the years. It is something to do with us as people, our personality, and our survival.

A friend of mine once told me that he knew his elderly father realized that his own death was approaching: he handed over his wallet and his cheque book to his wife. We only hand over our control—our independence—as a last resort.

———————

The Centurion sent friends with this message: Do not trouble further, sir . . . I know, for I am myself a man under orders, with soldiers under me . . .   (Luke 7: 6, 8)

———————

> Father, Lord of all,
> we acknowledge our need
> to be in control
> of our bodies,
> our actions,
> and of events which may fashion
> the course of our lives.
>
> Look graciously
> on those who suffer
> distress and anxiety
> when they feel they are losing control.
> Grant them
> confidence in people around them,
> and boldness to speak for themselves.
> Give to others
> openness and sensitivity
> to perceive and respond to their needs.
> We ask this for your name's sake.

LOSS OF BODY IMAGE ◈

G EORGINA was to undergo surgery which meant that she would lose her voice. Other people are more visibly changed through surgery or medical treatment. Some may lose a limb. Women may lose a breast. Others may be scarred around the head following brain surgery. People who have undergone radiotherapy may lose their hair. Those suffering from cancer may become emaciated or bloated due to the ravages of the disease.

Such changes are difficult to cope with. Our bodies are more than functional organisms enabling us to survive in our world. They are the vehicle of the personalities that we actually are. By the manner in which we dress and adorn our bodies, we express our personalities and how we relate, or wish to relate, to the world around us. Our bodies are constantly transmitting signals to, and receiving others from, people around us.

It is a sad blow, then, when our bodies, for reasons of illness, are no longer able to fulfil this function for us. We feel deprived, and, perhaps, lost. We feel we are not the people we used to be. We feel we have been reduced in our own estimation of ourselves and therefore, we assume, in the eyes of other people.

Fred was admitted for a colostomy operation. This was a blow to his self-esteem but the operation was a success, and the colostomy worked well. The most important factor in his recovery, however, was not physical. He needed to be reassured that his wife still loved him and was not put off or disgusted by his new condition. He needed to know that he was still, in her eyes, the man that she had married many years before.

God created human beings in his own image; in the image of God he created them.   (Genesis 1: 27)

He was despised, shunned by all, pain-racked and afflicted by disease . . . an object from which people turn away their eyes.   (Isaiah 53: 3)

Bearing the human likeness, sharing the human lot . . .   (Philippians 2: 7–8)

Father,
we give thanks
that you have called us
to be your people,
that you have fashioned us
in your image,
and that Jesus your Son
shared our human form and likeness.

Be close to all those
whose bodies are altered
   by sickness and disease
   by surgery
   by the effects of radical treatment.

Though they feel diminished
in their own eyes,
and others may find them
difficult to look upon,
may they be upheld and affirmed
by knowing that they are ever
infinitely perfect and acceptable
to you, the Creator and Maker of all.

'ROLLER-COASTER' ◈

I BAPTIZED Anthony when he was just a few days old. He had been born with a badly defective heart, and had been transferred to Guy's from his local hospital.

He underwent surgery on his heart, and was a long time in the intensive care unit. His condition varied enormously. Sometimes he made good progress and gave cause for great optimism. Sometimes he deteriorated and gave cause for grave concern. His parents were with him constantly, and both they and the unit staff shared all the variations in Anthony's condition.

At long last the day arrived when he had improved enough to go home, and hopes were high. Within a week or so he was back in Guy's. Again he improved. Again he went home, but only for a few days. Again he had to come back to hospital. His parents no longer knew what to hope for. It was, they said, like being on a giant roller-coaster. They had just climbed out of the bottom of the dive and regained their equilibrium, when down they went again. It was impossible to prepare themselves in any way, for they had no idea what might lie ahead. To talk about taking one day at a time was trite, and could bring them no comfort. The whole experience was nerve-racking, and it left them totally exhausted.

> They were carried up to the skies,
> then plunged down into the depths
>
> .   .   .   .   .   .
>
> So they cried to the Lord in their trouble,
> and he brought them out of their distress.
>
> (Psalm 107: 26, 28)

Father, we remember
that in his care for your people
Jesus knew deep sorrow and great joy.

We pray for all
who watch by the bedside of their loved one,
and are carried from high hopes
to deep anxiety.
Hear them as they cry to you
in their trouble.
Bring them, we pray,
out of their distress.
Grant them calmness and peace.
Be to them a haven
where they may know
the security of your presence,
and give thanks to you
for your enduring love.

THOSE IN DESPAIR ▩

You have crushed us . . . and covered us with deepest darkness.

(Psalm 44: 19)

THERE are some people who are overwhelmed by their illness and for whom the darkness is complete. One man I knew had had a major operation which not only involved his life expectancy but the quality of life as he had known it until then. He felt crushed and covered with deepest darkness. The faith, which had been an important feature of his life before the operation, completely deserted him. He had no feeling of the presence of God or even of his absence, nor did he feel able to make any purely intellectual assent—an act of will.

I tried using all the Christian imagery. I spoke of his experience in terms of death and resurrection. I used John 1: 5: 'The light shines in the darkness and the darkness has never mastered it.' From the psalms I quoted 88: 18: 'Darkness is now my only companion.' If he could regard darkness as a friend rather than an enemy, that at least would be something positive. Even the descent of Jesus into hell meant nothing to him.

I then tried a less religious approach. Had he experienced these feelings before? Did they reverberate on any previous experiences of loss? I assured him that, given the traumatic nature of his operation, his feelings were only to be expected. Eventually, I was forced to admit that I had nothing that apparently could bring him any glimmer of light or begin to lead him from the darkness. All I could do was to be with him and to pray for him—but not with him—and in some sense to share his darkness.

This, in fact, was unavoidable. His darkness was not only communicated to me, but to the many staff who looked after him. We all felt that we had failed him and that, despite our best efforts, we had not been able to achieve that positive outcome for which we had worked so hard.

Father of all goodness,
who commanded the light
to shine out of darkness,
be with all those
whose illness leads them
into depression and despair.
As they pass through
the valley of deepest darkness,
may they know
that you are with them.
Lead them and strengthen them,
and bring them to see
that your light
is never mastered or quenched,
the light of your glory
in the face of Jesus Christ.

Loving Father,
look in compassion
on all who care for people
depressed and brought low
through suffering and illness.

As their own wounds are touched
and painful memories revived,
grant to them wholeness
of person and purpose,
so that with patience, skill, and insight,
they may themselves
bring new vision and hope
to people in their care.

WHEN LIFE IS TOO MUCH ▣

'I THINK he's given up,' she said to me, standing by the bed of her deeply unconscious husband. 'He was all right until three weeks ago. Then he knew he'd got cancer, and there was nothing else they could do for him. He's just turned his face to the wall since then.'

She was probably right. I have known other people do the same thing, especially if they were elderly, and felt that they did not want invasive treatment in order to prolong their life for an uncertain and lonely future. They have preferred to 'turn their faces to the wall', and make as peaceful an exit as possible from life.

There are those whose exit, or attempted exit, is far less peaceful. On the day I write these words, I have read of a four-year-old child who hanged himself in his bedroom after being chastised by his mother. It is sadly not uncommon to hear of prisoners hanging themselves in their cells. People I have known in hospital have jumped out of an upstairs window, hanged themselves from the lavatory chain, slashed their wrists, jumped in front of a train. One locomotive driver I knew of had someone leap into the path of his train on two occasions. The first led to the amputation of both feet of the person concerned. The second incident was fatal. The driver's nerve was shattered, and he was unable to return to work for a long time.

Suicide, or attempted suicide, has a profound effect on others, and it is suggested that this is at least one of the reasons why people seek to take their own lives. Suicide can be an act of revenge, a show of aggression, or a cry for help. For people who are profoundly mentally ill, it can be a response to the inner voices which goad and taunt them. The common thread through all these tragic incidents is the feeling that life is too much.

You have taken friend and neighbour far from me; darkness is now my only companion.   (Psalm 88: 18)

A darkness fell over the whole land.   (Luke 23: 44)

The light shines in the darkness, and the darkness has never mastered it.   (John 1: 5)

———————

Lord Jesus,
as you bowed your head and died,
a great darkness covered the land.

We lay before you
the despair of all
who find life
without meaning or purpose,
and see no value in themselves,
who suffer the anguish
of inner darkness
that can only lead them
to self-destruction and death.

Lord,
in your passion, you too
felt abandoned, isolated, derelict.

You are one
with all who suffer
pain and torment
of body and mind.

Be to them the light
that has never been mastered.
Pierce the darkness
which surrounds and engulfs them,
so that they may know
within themselves
acceptance, forgiveness, and peace.

We pray for those who,
through the suicide
of one close to them,
suffer the emptiness of loss
and the burden of untold guilt.
May they know
your gift of acceptance,
so that they may be freed
from self-reproach
and mutual recrimination,
and find in the pattern
of your dying and rising,
new understanding, and purpose
for their lives.

LETTING GO ◈

'**D**o you think God would be angry with me?' asked one distraught young mother. Her son had been badly injured in a road accident and the decision had been jointly taken by parents and hospital staff that active treatment should be discontinued.

The bonding between the boy and his mother was particularly strong, so strong, in fact, that she was unable to contemplate life without him. She felt that she should end her own life in order to accompany him through death into the life to come. I replied that I believed that God would not be angry. He would be deeply sad, for the death of her son, for the injury, illness, or death of any of his children, and above all as he was for the death of Jesus, his own son.

Her father had died comparatively recently. She had enjoyed a close relationship with him and he had been close to the dead child. It was her father, we agreed, who could be relied on to welcome her son into the next world and look after him there. She herself was needed by her husband and family in the world here and now. This idea comforted her, and although the theology of it may be uncertain, it made sense to her.

After much talking along these lines, the mother was enabled to let go of her child. She held him with great calmness and tranquillity as treatment was discontinued, and death came swiftly and peacefully.

―――――――

'Do not cling to me,' said Jesus.   (John 20: 17)

Stay with us, for evening approaches, and the day is almost over.   (Luke 24: 29)

―――――――

Lord Jesus Christ,
crucified and risen,
your presence was precious
to Mary and the disciples.

We pray for all
who have been bereaved
of people they loved.
Help them to see
that in clinging to them
they lose them,
but in letting them go,
they open themselves
and their loved ones
to the fullness of life eternal
where all are one in your love,
now and evermore.

WHERE ARE THEY NOW? ▨

I WAS sitting with a young couple whose baby had died very quickly and unexpectedly. They had spent a lot a time with him since he died, and had been left by the staff to make their own goodbyes in their own time and in their own way. The time had now come for them to leave and register the child's death before they went back home, some distance away. I had been involved with them during the few days their child had been in Guy's, and I needed to take leave of them myself.

'So where do you think he is now?' The question was a big one. It came unexpectedly and caught me unawares. I could not avoid it and there was no time to think. I replied (if I remember correctly) that their child was in the nearer presence of God, and being held in the love of God. I added that the love of God is such that it straddles this world and the world to come. It is a link between the two, so that whether we are in this world or the world to come, we are kept in the same love of God. It also means that we have a permanent and indissoluble link with those who have gone before us because we are all one in God, and his love is greater than anything we can conceive or know.

I had to admit to the couple that I was seeking to put into words my beliefs, perhaps my feelings, about things which really defy being expressed in words. But I think that because I had not fobbed them off with religious language, and because I was obviously making an honest attempt to communicate, if not explain, one of the great mysteries of life, they got the feel of what I was saying and seemed to find it helpful. I hope so. At times like that, words seem of little use, and one has to rely on the images and pictures that it is possible to create.

For I am convinced that there is nothing in death or life—nothing in all creation . . . that can separate us from the love of God in Christ Jesus our Lord.   (Romans 8: 38, 39)

Father
we give thanks to you
for our belief
that through the death and resurrection
of our Lord Jesus Christ,
those who have died
are in your presence
and in your care,
which binds together
our world and the world unseen.

Be with all those
who mourn the loss
of one dear to them.
Help them to know
that they are always
one together in you,
for neither death nor life
can separate us
from the love
you have shared with us
in Jesus Christ,
your Son, our Lord.

UNFINISHED BUSINESS ◈

M Y father died twenty years ago of cancer. Slowly and uncomfortably, he became more and more incapacitated as his condition grew worse. He never spoke directly to the family of his increasing weakness, and we never mentioned it to him.

I was living some distance away at the time. I went to see him as often as I could, but not all that often. One day, at the end of my visit, as I got up from his bedside to leave, he asked me, totally unexpectedly, if there was anything else I wanted to say to him. He obviously knew he was dying and that we would not see each other again—something which I, despite my experience of hospital ministry, had not realized. His question took me completely by surprise. We had never found it easy to communicate, and now all I could answer was no. I left, and the moment was gone for ever. In retrospect, as the years have gone by, I realize that there was a great deal I wanted to say to him, and perhaps he to me.

But that would have meant daring to reveal our true feelings to one another and talking about them—which was something we had never managed to do. Perhaps neither of us would have coped with such a revelation at such a time, and it was better to leave things as they were.

Nevertheless, the moment is surrounded by deep regret on my part. The memory remains a painful one, although the passage of time has blurred the feeling of self-recrimination. The experience has taught me that if I have important things to say to people, I must make sure that I tell them—while there is still time.

Suddenly there were two men talking with Jesus—Moses and Elijah—who . . . spoke of his departure, the destiny he was to fulfil in Jerusalem.   (Luke 9: 30–1)

Jesus said, 'It is accomplished!' Then he bowed his head and gave up his spirit.   (John 19: 30)

———————

Lord Jesus Christ,
as you bowed your head
and gave up your Spirit,
you died with your destiny fulfilled,
and your mission accomplished.

Look in compassion on those
who mourn their loved ones
with deep regrets for matters uncompleted:
goodbyes to be said;
past hurts forgiven;
misunderstandings put right;
explanations given.

Grant them in their sadness
peace of mind,
freedom from guilt, reproach,
and self-recrimination,
and the knowledge that all,
whether in this life or beyond,
are one with you,
and with each other,
through your unfailing love.

HEALING PAST HURTS ◈

O N the bed lay a teddy bear, so obviously brand new, that I could not help remarking on it. Joan told me the story. She had a brother who was six years older. When they were children, he teased her by doing all sorts of things to her favourite teddy bear—like hanging him out of the bedroom window on the end of a string. The final 'trick' was to cut off all his hair and place him on top of the bonfire on Guy Fawkes night.

When Joan was admitted to hospital her brother came to see her. In his hand was a parcel which he presented to her. As soon as she felt it, she knew immediately what it was—and why.

On one level it was a light-hearted gesture to cheer her up in the face of serious illness. On another, deeper level, it was an outward sign of the desire to put things right. Many of us feel the need to heal past hurts, and the major events of life often serve to concentrate our minds, and push us into action.

> Lord Jesus
> you taught us to pray
> for the forgiveness of the wrong
> that we have done,
> as we have forgiven
> those who have wronged us.
>
> Help us also to forgive ourselves
> for moments we can never forget,
>   deeds we can never undo,
>   words we can never take back,
>   things we bitterly regret.
> As we look back in sorrow,

help us also to look forward in joy,
knowing that past wrongs can be righted,
and pain and hurt healed
in your name and for your sake.

TEARS ▧

THE gospels tell us that tears were an integral part of the life and ministry of Jesus. Mary, his mother, was told that sorrow, like a sharp sword, would pierce her heart.

The widow of Nain wept for her dead son, and Mary and Martha for their brother Lazarus when he died.

Mary Magdalene wept over the feet of Jesus in the home of Simon the leper and outside his tomb in the Garden of Gethsemane.

In bitter remorse, Peter wept for shame that he had three times denied that he knew Jesus. The city of Jerusalem also rejected Jesus, and caused him to weep tears of great anguish. The death of his friend Lazarus also brought him deep sorrow. 'Jesus wept.'

> Father we offer to you
> the tears shed in hospital:
>
> The tears of parents for their dying child,
> the anguish of cot-death,
> and the anger against the drunken driver.
>
> The tears of families losing a loved one,
> the fears of those who do not want to die,
> the frustrations of those who do,
> but whose time has not yet come.
>
> The tears brought by bad news,
> and the anxieties of waiting.
> Tears caused by pain,
> and the results of major surgery.
> The tears of those who watch,
> and of those who can only wait.

The tears of hospital staff:
>the junior doctor who experiences
>the limitations of time and resources,
>the senior nurse who acknowledges
>her own vulnerability.

But Father, not all tears in hospital are sad.
We give thanks
>for the tears of parents who gaze
>in awe and wonder
>at their new-born child;
>for the tears of those who realize anew
>the upholding love and affection
>of their family and friends;
>for the tears of those who,
>recovering from their illness,
>go on their way rejoicing;
>for the tears of those whose hearts
>are filled with love and gratitude
>towards you:
>for the tears of those who feel
>unable to express their emotions
>in any other way.

Father, as Jesus wept, we pray
>That you will accept through him
>the tears of all those who weep.

ACTS OF FAITH ◈

D OROTHY was an elderly lady whose spiritual home lay
within the conservative Anglo-Catholic tradition. She
liked to receive the sacrament frequently and regularly
while she was in hospital for a long course of treatment. She told
me that each time she received Holy Communion it was for her a
renewal of her act of faith that God would heal her from her illness.
She was a sociable and lively person and related well to other
patients on the ward. Because her faith was very real to her, she saw
it as a means to support and help one of the other ladies who was
going through a particularly bad spell, when everything seemed to
be going wrong, and the whole fabric of her life falling apart.

By contrast, Elaine was a regular patient on the oncology ward.
Her admissions were frequent though they varied in length of
time. I had seen her on previous visits but without any significant
conversation taking place. This particular day she was keen to talk.
She talked at length about her illness, her feelings about it, and her
lack of religious belief. She had never been a church-goer, and the
little belief she had held had disappeared as her illness became
more serious and recurrent. 'But', she said 'you've got to have
faith, you've got to put your confidence in something.' It was
important to her that she should have confidence in her doctors,
and that they knew what they were doing. She needed to have
confidence in the nurses, whom she knew and liked, that they
would look after her well, and meet her needs. She needed to have
confidence in her husband and family, that no matter what the
ravages of her illness might be, she would be loved and supported
by them. She needed to have confidence in herself that she would
be able to stay the course, and go on fighting the illness as long as
she could.

Even though she could not manage to make the leap of faith herself, it was not difficult for me to translate what she was saying into a religious framework. It seemed to me that in spite of what she said, Elaine was not far from the kingdom of God.

God is my deliverer.
I am confident and unafraid

(Isaiah 12: 2)

When Jesus saw how thoughtfully he answered, he said to him, 'You are not far from the Kingdom of God.'   (Mark 12: 34)

**God our loving Father,
you are a refuge and stronghold,
a timely help in trouble.**

**We bring to you
all whose lives are beset
by accident or illness.**

**We give thanks for those
who are confident and unafraid,
and believe in you as their deliverer.**

**We pray for those
who find it difficult to believe.**

**Grant to them all, strength in their weakness,
and rest in their weariness.**

**Encourage them to cast aside doubts and fears
so that they may believe in themselves,
have confidence in those who care for them,
and rest secure in you
and in your love made known to us
through Jesus Christ our Lord.**

HOPING AGAINST HOPE ◈

S TEVE lay in the intensive care unit, desperately ill. He had suffered nearly fifty heart attacks within the previous three days. His chest was still red, bearing livid testimony to the efforts of those who had resuscitated him yet once more. He was on the life-support machine, and, it seemed, every other piece of apparatus that could possibly be used to maintain and promote his failing grasp on life.

His young wife stood on one side of his bed, I on the other. 'I know he's going to get better. You are, Steve, aren't you—for my sake.' The body remained inert. There was not so much as a flicker of the eyelids. The life-support machine maintained its rhythmic pumping. She turned to me. 'I've got to believe he's going to get better. I've got to go on hoping.'

It is a matter of pastoral judgement as to how far people like Sally should be supported in their hope. To deny them all hope would be cruel and shattering, but equally to encourage them to an unrealistic degree would only serve to make the pain of loss and separation harder to bear in the end.

As we have ultimately to let go of the dead or dying person, so in these circumstances we have gradually to let go of hope. Hope is relinquished as we accept that death must inevitably come.

———

There are three things that last forever: Faith, hope, and love.   (1 Corinthians 13: 13)

If it is for this life only that Christ has given us hope, we of all people are most to be pitied.   (1 Corinthians 15: 19)

———

Loving Father,
the source of all truth and all hope;
we pray for all
who are confronted
by the loss of those they love,
who find the truth
difficult to accept,
and who flee from reality
into hoping against hope.

As mortal hope recedes,
we pray that they may find strength
in your abiding hope
that nothing can separate us
from your presence,
for in you
life is stronger than death itself,
as you have shown us
in your Son, Jesus Christ our Lord.

TRUTH AND FREEDOM ◈

You will know the truth, and the truth will set you free.

(John 8: 32)

MIKE, one of our Chaplaincy visitors at Guy's, was telling us in a team meeting about an encounter he had had with an old lady on one of the care of the elderly wards. She was well into her eighties, but her faculties were as sharp as ever. 'They want to take my leg off,' she had said to Mike. 'But I'm all right.'

As a chaplaincy team we savoured those words, and the feelings they conveyed. Here was an old lady, full of character and determination. She appreciated fully both the situation and all its implications. She knew that medically she needed an operation in order to save her life. But she also felt that she had lived as long as she wanted. She was not interested in prolonging her life if it meant surgery, pain and discomfort in hospital, and a complete change of life-style after she was discharged. She was not ungrateful, but she was being realistic. She, as it were, 'knew the score'. The words of Jesus express her feelings more significantly: 'You will know the truth, and the truth will set you free.'

> **Father**
> **we give thanks to you**
> **for all who have seen**
> **the vision of your truth,**
> **and who have received thereby**
> **the gracious gift of freedom.**
>
> **Be with all**
> **who know the truth about**
> **their health and their illness.**
> **Guide them in their decisions**

by the light of your truth.
In your light may they see light,
and find the blessing
of healing and peace.

DEPENDENCE AND DETERMINATION ▣

'How are you?' I asked, as I introduced myself and sat down. Her eyes immediately filled with tears. 'I've lost the use of my legs,' she replied. 'They just won't go at all.' She went on to explain what had happened. She had had treatment for cancer some years previously, but had been well up to four weeks before I saw her. One day her legs had simply seized up, and she had been unable to move. Intensive physiotherapy had restored at least some of the movement, and she had also been provided with a wheelchair. 'But I'm an active person,' she protested. 'I'm always busy doing something or the other. Now I've got to rely on other people to do for me so many of the things I want to do for myself. But I shouldn't grizzle like this. There's no use being sorry for yourself. I've got great determination. I've made up my mind I'm going to walk again—and I will.'

I replied that in no way should she regard her tears as a sign of weakness. They were a natural response to the loss of her independence, and all that it meant to her. I encouraged her determination to walk again. Despite her tears she had a glint in her eye, and I remarked upon it. I knew she would walk again if she could, and she probably would.

Father, in your compassion
look on all
who lose their independence
through illness.

Grant them
> patience to accept their condition;
> tolerance with themselves;
> gratitude towards others;
> determination to overcome their disability;
> strength to persevere.

Grant to those who look after them
foresight and imagination,
and the spirit of service,
without condescension,
after the pattern of your Son,
Jesus Christ our Lord.

PATIENTS AND PATIENCE ◈

T HE noun 'patient' is derived from the Latin verb meaning to suffer. 'Patience' by extension is defined as 'calm endurance of hardship, provocation, pain, delay, etc. . . . the capacity for calm self-possessed waiting'.

In hospital, patients need patience. The system may work slowly and it can be irksome waiting for something to happen or a member of staff to arrive. An irate husband rang a Senior Nurse to ask why his wife's newspaper had not been delivered to the ward by mid-morning. On the other hand, the wait may be for much more important things. The arrival of the doctor may herald good news or bad. The results of tests may involve important and far-reaching decisions. The long-awaited moment is dreaded as well as anticipated. In one sense it cannot come soon enough. In another, it comes all too soon. Either way, the effects of the moment have to be taken on board, assimilated, coped with, acted upon.

Families and relatives also suffer, and also need patience. I happened to meet a mother and father, sitting and waiting while their child was undergoing an operation. They had gone with him to the operating theatre, said goodbye to him, handed him over, and come back to the ward knowing the possibility that they might never see him alive again. Happily he recovered, but their waiting is not over. Having survived one operation, the child now faces a further series. In a sense, their waiting has only just begun.

For another woman, her waiting is over, and was in vain. Her husband had a major operation for a serious heart condition. Routinely he was taken from theatre into intensive care. However, it was obvious things were going wrong. The life-supporting technology increased as his body ceased to cope with the demands made upon it. His wife waited at his bedside every day and most nights. Finally, when he died, she found consolation in the fact that she had waited patiently beside him and had been with him at the moment of his death. In that way, she felt, she had shared his suffering. The fact that she had lost trace of the passage of time during that period was not important.

> Father
>> all time is yours,
>> yet in your Son,
>> you entered our world of time,
>> and were subject to all its demands.
>
> Be with all those in hospital
>> who wait for staff to arrive;
>> treatment to be given;
>> results of tests;
>> recovery of health;
>> and who watch by the bedside
>> of someone they love.
>
> When time for them loses its meaning
>>> its shape
>>> its feel
> may they know that you are with them,
>> the Lord of all time,
> and that as they live each moment
>> of the time that you have given them
>> they are precious in your sight.

ASKING QUESTIONS ⊗

'CAN you manage to wash yourself?' the nurse asked an elderly lady suffering from arthritis, just one of the conditions for which she had been admitted to hospital. It was a standard question, typical of all those that are asked of patients every day by various members of staff. Personal details have to be asked, significant information has to be sought so that a diagnosis can be made, a course of treatment decided upon, and the most suitable and appropriate care offered to each patient. This will vary according to the personality, family background, and circumstances of each and every individual.

If questions have to be asked of patients, then equally patients have questions which they need to put to hospital staff. Some questions will be basic, simply requesting information about how the hospital functions. Most will be more searching, requesting information regarding the nature of the illness, the progress of the illness, and its likely outcome. Other questions may be deeper and more far-reaching, seeking to make sense of the situation in which the patient finds him/herself: 'Why should this illness happen? What have I done to bring this about?' As one patient said to me, 'My guilt level seems to be going up and up and up.'

In a setting where questions are almost a way of life, it is essential that they should be asked sensitively and tactfully, and answered as frankly and truthfully as possible. That entails creating an environment where people, both patients and staff, can feel confident to be open and honest with each other.

And after three days [his parents] found him sitting in the temple surrounded by the teachers, listening to them and putting questions. (Luke 2: 46)

'Tell us', they said, 'by what authority you are acting like this . . .?' Jesus answered them, 'I also have a question for you . . .' (Luke 20: 2–3)

Lord Jesus Christ,
during your life among us
you were asked many questions,
and yourself asked many in return.

Be present with all
who ask questions in hospital:
staff and patients.
Give gentleness to those who seek information
        tact to those who give it
            courage to those who receive it.

Grant them confidence
that in sharing knowledge about themselves,
they are drawing close to you,
the source of our knowledge of the love of God,
and of his care for us all.

BAD NEWS ▨

ONE day I met three people who had just received bad news. In each instance, the news was of a life-threatening illness.

One lady had been admitted to hospital for what she expected would be an investigation for a chest complaint. She discovered that she had a malignant growth on one kidney and that the other had been rendered useless by medication taken over many years for rheumatism.

The second lady came back as an out-patient for a check-up following a long stay in hospital. She had been admitted for treatment of a skin condition which had been so severe that it had affected her heart and her lungs. Now she had been told that the damage was irreparable and that her only chance of survival lay in a heart-lung transplant.

A third lady was already receiving extended treatment for cancer. Just before I arrived on the ward, she had been told that there was now, according to the latest X-ray, 'a patch on her lung'. The implications were obvious.

The first lady was stunned by the seriousness of the news. The test had been a painful one and she was still feeling the after-effects, but the enormity of the situation overwhelmed her, and she was very depressed. When she rallied a little, it was to feel angry with those who had advised her medically. To have cancer on one kidney was bad enough, but to find that the other was not functioning because of medication which had been prescribed, and which she had innocently and faithfully taken, was really too awful to contemplate. Her spirits were too low even for her to feel angry enough for her to project her feelings on to her GP, the hospital—or God. 'The others haven't been much use,' she said, 'let's see if God can do something.'

The other two ladies reacted differently. They had both been in hospital for a long time, and both knew that they were, or had been, seriously ill. Therefore they were over the initial stage of shock. Perhaps it was this experience which led them to deny the worst prognosis, and at a simplistic level, to hope for the best. The second lady said, 'I feel so much better now. If I can go on like this I'm sure I shall be all right.' The third said, 'I know my breathing's not too good but I put it down to this hot weather we're having at the moment.'

Both of them were communicating that reality was, for the moment, too painful to bear. Sadly they were also communicating the wish for reality to disappear. If they denied it hard enough and long enough, maybe the unpalatable truth would fade away, and be turned into the good news which they longed to hear.

> Lord Jesus,
> When you came to the place called Gethsemane, you
> were almost crushed by the sorrow in your heart.

> Let your compassion uphold those
>   who also feel crushed
>   by the weight of their sorrow:
>   the shock of bad news;
>   their disbelief and denial;
>   the possibility that life may be ending soon;
>   their anxiety for other people and for themselves.

> Face to face with their mortality
> May they find strength in your eternity.

God our Father,

The false prophets were condemned for crying
    'Peace, peace', where there was no peace.

Be with all those who, in the course of their duty,
    have to be bearers of bad news.

Enable them so to speak the truth with love,
    that those who receive their words
    may find
    that their burden is lightened
    that their hope is not quenched
    and that they can draw strength
    from knowing
    that the truth can set us free.

ANXIETY ▧

MANY years ago, a leading consultant referred to hospitals, in general, as being 'a cradle of anxiety'. This expressive phrase has not been bettered in the intervening years. A hospital is a place where anxiety abounds, so much so that it is impossible to begin to make any list of the people who are anxious, and what their anxieties are. Many of them have already appeared in the pages of this book. More will follow subsequently.

Anxiety can be a good thing. It can alert us to the fact that things are not as they should be or how we would want them to be, so we need to take action in order to bring about a change in the situation. Too often, however, anxiety is negative. For whatever reason, we feel prevented from taking action, or have to hand over a situation to other people to act on our behalf. Or we may be troubled about the outcome of a situation which affects us or the people we love. We may fear bad news, or our lives may have been shattered by sudden tragedy. All this can be emotionally distressing and physically debilitating. It is anxiety at its worst.

So do not be anxious about tomorrow; tomorrow will look after itself. Each day has troubles enough of its own.   (Matthew 6: 34)

Father,
we are familiar
with the words of Jesus,
yet we have to confess
that we find it difficult
to make them our own.

Look in your mercy
Upon all in anxiety
    for those whom they love,
    for themselves,
    about the outcome of the morrow.
Reassure them with the knowledge
that you are with them at all times,
And that day by day
they are held in your love.

UNCERTAINTY ▨

A LOCAL vicar rang me to ask if I could provide him with any more information regarding the progress of one of his parishioners who had been an in-patient at Guy's for a long time. The man's wife was becoming more and more distraught with the pressure of coping with family life alone and the long separation from her husband. The vicar wanted to be able to offer her support and reassurance, but he could not do that realistically, as he said, without the basis of some firm knowledge.

I managed to go to the ward at the time when the woman was visiting her husband. She was obviously very much on edge and on the brink of tears. 'If only I knew what was going to happen,' she said. 'It's the uncertainty that gets me down.'

The feeling of uncertainty is difficult and debilitating, not only for families but for hospital staff as well. My years as a hospital chaplain have witnessed a constant series of changes in the structure and organization of the hospitals in which I have worked. As I write, Guy's and St Thomas's are being united in a single NHS Trust. A new strategy is being worked out for the rationalization of the provision of health care across the capital. There is much speculation as to what the shape of the new service might be. There is much unease amongst hospital staff as to whether there will be a place for them within it, or whether they will be facing redundancy. Uncertainty abounds.

From the end of the earth I call to you with fainting heart;
lift me up and set me high on a rock.

(Psalm 61: 2)

The Lord of Hosts is with us;
the God of Jacob is our fortress.

(Psalm 46: 7)

Jesus then said to his disciples, 'Let us go back to Judaea.' 'Rabbi,' his disciples said, 'it is not long since the Jews there were wanting to stone you. Are you going there again? . . .' Thomas, called 'the Twin', said to his fellow-disciples, 'Let us also go and die with him.' (John 11: 7–8, 16)

Lord God,
we remember the uncertainty of the disciples
as they followed Jesus,
not knowing where he would lead them
or what the outcome might be.

We commend to you
all who face the uncertainty
of the outcome of their illness,
of the illness of their loved ones,
of the organization of the hospitals in which they work.
Be to them always a strong rock,
and a source of strength,
and in the midst
of uncertainty and change,
grant them the assurance
of your unchanging presence.

ETHICAL QUESTIONS ◈

I RECEIVED a telephone call from the genetics department. Would I be willing to see a couple who were coming to the department for genetic counselling? The wife was pregnant but a scan had shown that her baby was badly deformed, and she was being offered a termination. She was undecided but her husband had strong religious views, and was not prepared to contemplate an abortion under any circumstances.

I fixed a place and time to see them, but I was left wondering whether there was a hidden agenda. Would the couple be coming to talk with me so that they could discuss their doubts and indecision in a religious context away from the genetics department? Was the department hoping that either I might put pressure on the husband, or give him some kind of religious dispensation so that he would change his mind, and give permission for the termination to take place?

The more I thought about the question, the more I realized how many far-reaching issues were involved. I had no information about the couple. I did not know whether they had any other children or what might be the effect upon them if a handicapped child were born into the family. On the other hand, what would be the effect on the couple if the foetus were aborted? It seemed that they were already in some degree of conflict. If the termination took place, the conflict might become worse, even to the extent of the total breakdown of the relationship. If the baby were to be born severely handicapped, would the family manage to look after the child? What outside resources would be necessary? Would they be available? If so, who would pay for them? What would be the cost in the long term to the community as a whole, of preserving the life of this child? We agree that human life is of infinite value and worth, but can that argument always be sustained in a world of finite resources? Indeed, should the argument be sustained? How does a hospital or community use its resources? How does it make its decision? On what criteria are decisions taken? Who makes the decisions—and on what authority?

Questions abound. There are no easy answers or even ready answers. In some instances, there appear to be no answers at all. Yet decisions have to be made. Often they have to be made quickly, without time and opportunity for considered judgement. It is at such times that wisdom and experience are at a premium. It is no use being wise with hindsight. We have to live with the results and consequences of our decision.

> Make us know how few are our days,
> that our minds may learn wisdom.
>
> (Psalm 90: 12)

When the Spirit of truth comes, he will guide you into all the truth.   (John 16: 13)

> **Lord God the Holy Spirit,**
> **source of all wisdom and truth,**
> **we pray that you will guide**
> **all those who have to take decisions**
> **with far-reaching consequences**
> > **for people in their care,**
> > **in the use of valuable resources,**
> > **on the life of the hospital.**
> **Grant them the gift of wisdom.**
> **Enable them to discern truth,**
> **so that amid confusion and conflict,**
> **they may be able to choose the better way**
> **for all concerned,**
> **and be at peace in themselves,**
> **and with you.**

SPACE ▣

THE concept of personal space is one which is well known to counsellors, therapists, and anyone who studies the expressions of body language. Hospitals are required to provide each patient with a specified minimum amount of space around their bed.

Curtains provide a line of demarcation and a flimsy protection. The bed-space is constantly invaded by a stream of people from cleaners to consultants. At other times it is taken over by numbers of visitors.

To be aware of this will provide us with the tact and sensitivity we need to rescue us from the assumption that we are always welcome, in whatever capacity we come. Usually we are—but it is only courtesy to ask.

———

Very early next morning Jesus got up and went out. He went away to a remote spot and remained there in prayer.   (Mark 1: 35)

———

> **God of all creation**
> **and Lord of all space:**
> **We remember that your son**
> **our Lord Jesus Christ**
> **retired to lonely places**
> **to be by himself.**
>
> **Thank you for giving us**
> **the space that we need.**

Help us to be sensitive to the needs
of all who are in hospital,
to respect their privacy,
and to preserve their space,
so that they may be themselves
and find space for you.

'THE MAGIC WAND' ◈

'I DON'T know why I asked to see you,' she said. 'I don't know what to say or what I want to talk to you about.' I had been called to the cardiac ward late one evening. Sister told me over the phone that she had a lady who was first on the list for major heart surgery the following morning. The lady was extremely anxious, and had expressed a wish to see the chaplain.

The start of my conversation with Nancy was not promising. Once she began talking, however, it became clear that she suffered from a wide range of problems, not the least of which was that she had, in her own words, a morbid fear of death. Her operation had been fully explained to her, and she rather wished now she had not asked for all the details. She wanted someone—the surgeons, nurses, her family, me, anyone—to give her a cast-iron guarantee that the operation would be successful, and that she would not die during the course of it or as a result of it. Yet she knew that this was impossible and, in any case, her rational self would not have believed it had anyone tried to give her some form of guarantee.

She was not a religious person, and had no connection with any of the churches. So I asked her why she had asked for me to come. 'I don't really know,' she said, 'I just felt that if I was able to talk it might make things better. What I really want is for you to wave the magic wand, and make it all come right.' I did not need to point out that I had no magic wand and in fairness to her, she did not expect me to have one. There was no time to deal with her problems, but I wanted to give her something positive to hold on to. I pointed out to her that she had already faced and overcome many difficulties in her life, and that she could bring those same resources to bear in facing her operation. In this sense, the operation could mark something of a milestone or even a turning-point in her life. I remembered the old saying, 'Tomorrow is the first day of the rest of your life.' It was trite, but it appealed to her, and it was certainly more positive than talking about the magic wand. She repeated the words, thanked me for coming—and went off to the landing by the lifts to light up another cigarette.

When Herod saw Jesus he was greatly pleased; he had heard about him and had long been wanting to see him in the hope of witnessing some miracle performed by him.   (Luke 23: 8)

> So they cried to the Lord in their trouble
> and he rescued them from their distress.
>
> (Psalm 107: 6)

Heavenly Father,
in your compassion
look on all who call to you
in fear, anxiety, and distress of mind.
Grant them to know that you are with them.
Strengthen them within
so that with confidence
they may be able to withstand
all the stresses which beset them,
and grant them your peace
which passes all understanding;
in the name of Jesus Christ our Lord.

THE GIFT OF HEALING ▦

THE gift of healing has enjoyed a much greater emphasis in the life of the Churches over the last few years. For too long it was a gift which had been largely forgotten and neglected. The ministry of healing was kept alive by the work and effort of a few specialist societies and fellowships. Inevitably, healing became their preserve.

The influence of charismatic renewal has changed the situation dramatically. Healing has been rediscovered, and is recognized once more as one of the gifts of the Spirit. The ministry of healing is widely practised. Healing services are held in all kinds of places and situations, which may vary from exuberant evangelistic meetings to the quiet laying-on of hands at the midday Eucharist in Westminster Abbey. The rediscovery of the gift of healing can only be good, and is a great blessing to the Christian community as a whole.

However, I have one regret. By and large the Church has allowed the gift of healing to follow the medical model. That is to say, someone falls ill. They consult their doctor who makes a diagnosis, and usually prescribes some form of medication to hasten their recovery. So often the Church follows the same pattern in its healing ministry, pursuing the same object, recovery or cure.

Of course it is possible to point to the example of Jesus as narrated in the Gospels, and the healing miracles which he performed. But it seems unlikely that Jesus ever 'simply' cured someone so that they were only restored to physical health. He touched them not only physically, but spiritually, so that their lives were redirected, their disease was overcome and put behind them. This profound reorientation does not form the basis of many of our prayers. They seem to concentrate on recovery and cure rather than on healing. Curing and healing are by no means one and the same.

Healing is about inner well-being, and the ability to establish good and satisfying relationships with other people. It may be the lack of such emotional and spiritual foundations which lead people in the first place to suffer from disease. It is significant that the words health, healing, and wholeness all derive from the same Germanic root.

None of this is new, but needs to be said again within the context of this book for the sake of completeness. Our prayer for healing may or may not include cure and/or recovery. Sometimes in the case of terminal illness or fatal injury, that is impossible to pray for. But we can always pray that a person may be healed. We can pray that they may know wholeness within themselves, may be content to be at one with God, with those whom they love, with the wider circle of friends and people around them, and so at one with themselves. This knowledge of wholeness is nourishing and sustaining. As we pray it for others, we pray it also for ourselves.

Jesus went round all the towns and villages teaching in their synagogues, proclaiming the good news of the kingdom, and curing every kind of illness and infirmity . . . Then he called his twelve disciples to him and gave them authority to drive out unclean spirits and to cure every kind of illness and infirmity.   (Matthew 9: 35; 10: 1)

> **Almighty God,**
> **the giver of all good gifts,**
> **we rejoice especially**
> **in your gift of healing,**
> **renewed and rediscovered**
> **within your Church.**

We give thanks for all
who practise this ministry,
and all who benefit by it.

Grant them cure and recovery
from illness of mind and body.
Grant them above all
the healing which comes
from the knowledge of your presence,
the assurance of your love,
and trust in your forgiveness and acceptance.
May they know they are one with you,
and with those whom they know and love.
So, at peace with themselves,
may they know your healing power.

A Prayer for Healing

May the Father who created you
restore you in his own image.
May the Son who died and rose again for you
grant you the assurance of his forgiveness.
May the Spirit who guides you
lead you to relationships
renewed and made whole.
May God the holy Trinity
bless you with his gift
of healing and peace.

RECOVERY FROM ILLNESS ▨

ALEX recovered from his operation and was transferred from intensive care back to the ward. I went to say goodbye to him before he returned home, and asked him what his thoughts and feelings were as he looked back on his time in hospital. He replied that he had been aware of two things which were especially important to him: first, that it had been a time of affection, and, secondly, that it had been a time of gifts. He was still too close to the experience to define it more precisely, but I understood what he meant. He was aware of the affection which had surrounded him from his wife, who had stayed in hospital with him, his family, the other patients, and the hospital staff. He was aware of the feeling of being buoyed up by the prayers of his friends and the whole congregation at his local church. It was obvious from his bedside locker that he had received many gifts but Alex meant more than that. He was aware that many people had used their various gifts on his behalf which, in their different ways, had aided his recovery.

But, as an outsider, I believe that a third very important quality had made its mark on his time in hospital. I believe that for him it had been a time of personal growth. He had become aware of new gifts and uncharted areas of understanding within himself. This had expressed itself in a visible deepening of his personal faith, and a willingness to grapple with the paradoxes and perplexities of the Christian faith as a whole. He was able to do this in the knowledge that he was held secure in the love of God expressed through the warmth and affection of his wife, family, and those who were caring for him.

Heavenly Father,
we praise you for all
who have recovered from their illness.
May they know
that you are the source of all healing,
and with grateful hearts
give themselves in love and service
to one another and to you,
in your name and for your sake.

BUT . . . ▧

EDNA had undergone major surgery. Several of her internal organs had been removed, and she had been given a stoma—an opening in the wall of the abdomen through which her bodily waste would now be evacuated and collected in a bag attached to her side.

I arrived as usual on Sunday morning to give her Holy Communion. She was obviously extremely upset and needed to talk. She said that she felt that she should have made a quicker recovery from her operation, even though it had been performed only ten days previously. She felt that she was not trying hard enough, and was determined to do better for the sake of her husband and family.

I tried to reassure her that she had in fact done very well, and that she was making a good recovery from a major operation, especially considering that it had been performed so recently. She simply burst into tears and sobbed, 'I saw it for the first time this morning.' I realized how far wide of the mark my response had been, and acknowledged this to her. The surgeons, nurses, stoma sister, and myself, could only answer her questions and seek to reassure her on a rational level. We could not ultimately enter her world and share her feelings about so many uncertainties. What did the future hold? Would she be able to cope with her bag? How would she feel about herself? What difference would this make to her relationships? What kind of person would she be? In spite of our best efforts, the big 'but . . .' remained.

My Father, if it is possible, let this cup pass me by.   (Matthew 26: 39)

Heavenly Father,
you are perfect in truth and love.
In Jesus, your son,
you entered our world
where fear and anxiety abound.
Be with all those who are full of doubt
about themselves,
about their illness,
and what the future holds.

Grant them to know
that you accept them,
love them, and hold them.
So may they believe in you,
and in themselves,
that their doubts trouble them no more,
and they rest secure in you.

I CAN'T BELIEVE IT ◈

TUESDAY morning. I am extremely anxious about the
middle-aged lady to whom I was due to give Communion
on Sunday. I went to her twice, but both times she was
drowsy, extremely short of breath, and not physically well enough
to make the effort to receive the sacrament. Monday had been my
day off, so on Tuesday morning I felt I must go to the ward again
to see how she was.

When I got there, the curtains were drawn. It was obvious
someone had died and I felt that my worst fears had been
confirmed. I was wrong. The lady I had been so concerned about
had made a dramatic recovery, and had been discharged on
Monday. But the rest of the ward was plunged into deep mourning
for a young woman in her late twenties who had been a patient for
some weeks, and had suddenly died at breakfast time.

In the bed opposite was another young woman who was one of
my regular communicants. She also had been a patient for some
while, and the two young women had grown close to one another
during their time on the ward. I went behind the curtains drawn
round her bed, and found her distraught. She was weeping
copiously as was the nurse who was trying to comfort her. I sat
with her, and in between her tears, she talked of the friend she had
lost. 'I just can't believe it,' she said. 'We waved goodnight to each
other last night as we had done so many times and she seemed OK.
And now she's gone. It's so final. I could have believed it if it had
been Gladys in the next bed [Gladys was eighty-seven], but not her.
She's so young. I just can't believe it.' I stayed with her some
while, and we talked together until her husband arrived.

The textbooks tell us of the shock and numbness which sudden
death causes in those who are bereaved. They are unable or

unwilling to take in the catastrophe that has occurred. There was a classic situation confronting me on the ward that morning.

———

Jesus . . . came to the disciples and found them asleep, worn out by grief.   (Luke 22: 45)

Mary stood outside the tomb weeping.   (John 20: 11)

———

Father
look in your compassion
upon all who are overcome
by shock and disbelief
at the loss of someone close to them,
and who find it difficult to accept
the emptiness that death can bring.

Be near to them
in their moment of anguish,
and sustain them
in the grief which lies ahead.

In the tumult of their feelings
may they know the strength of your love,
and find within themselves
acceptance and peace.

OUR OWN MORTALITY ◼

I HAVE been with many people when they have died. I have seen even more when they are dead. I have ministered to countless people in bereavement, and taken an untold number of funerals. I have gained an understanding of the dynamics of bereavement and loss, and spoken about them frequently on various occasions.

People who have been bereaved sometimes say to me, 'You've seen so much of this. I expect you're used to it all.' The first part of that remark is true. The second part is not. I never get used to suffering, bereavement, and the pain of human loss. I think that must be true of all hospital staff. If we ever 'get used to it', we are denying our vulnerability. What is worse, we have lost sight of our own mortality.

Every death with which I am involved reminds me that, one day, I too must die. Each grieving family to whom I minister reminds me that one day, I must take leave of those whom I love and those who love me. I have seen death often enough to recognize its essential aloneness. It is something we must accomplish by ourselves, no matter how many people are with us. The trained, professional part of me, the priest and pastor, tells me that there is nothing to fear, that I can confidently and fearlessly commit myself to God. The other part of me, that recognizes my own true feelings, is not so sure and acknowledges fears within.

Such is the sense of my own mortality which defies theological rationalization. Because I am aware of it, I avoid giving glib answers to the profound questions which people ask at times of anxiety and loss. Nor do I belittle their attempts to make sense of situations which defy all explanation. I could so easily be sitting one day where they are sitting now. Would I be coping any better, faced with questions of life and death? The sobering thought of our own mortality earths all our pastoral ministry to people in need.

Father
you have made us for yourself
and accept us in Jesus, your Son.

Give us your grace
to recognize within ourselves
anxieties about many things,
feelings of loss, of aloneness
and, at the last, the fear of death.

Enable us to use
what we see within us
as resources for our ministry,
so that we may come to you
with others in their need,
and together with them
lay before you our fears,
find strength to match our weakness,
and know your presence
when we feel most alone.

GIVING PERMISSION ▣

THE phone rang, rousing me out of a deep sleep. It was 4.30 a.m. The switchboard put me through to one of the night sisters who told me that a lady had died on one of the care of the elderly wards. The family were with her and would like me to go and say some prayers.

They were waiting for me when I arrived. There were five sons, two daughters, and two daughters-in-law. I talked with them briefly to get some kind of background to the situation. The mother was in her early seventies, and had died from cancer. Her death was expected, and the family had wanted to be with her when she died. They had tried their best, but as these things so often turn out, it had not been possible. They were not a religious family, and had no Church connection but they wanted me to say some prayers. I did this as we went on to the ward and gathered round the mother's bedside behind closed curtains. We thanked the staff nurse in charge of the ward who had handled the situation very sympathetically. I expressed my condolences to the family once more—my own mother had died fairly recently so I knew what they would be feeling. Then we went our separate ways.

As I drove home, I reflected on whether my journey had been really necessary. What had I achieved by saying prayers with the dead woman? The family, by their own admission, were not religious, so what had they really been asking for? I felt there were probably two things.

First, they needed to relieve a sense of guilt. They had not been able to be with their mother when she died, and felt bad about not being able to carry out their own good intentions.

Secondly, leading on from that, having arrived too late, they felt bad about leaving. They needed reassurance that it was acceptable for them to do so when there was nothing else they could do, or usefully achieve by staying. What I was able to offer was a formal taking leave of their mother, and some kind of official permission that they could now go home.

Heavenly Father,
you are closer to us
than we are to ourselves,
and know all the secrets of our hearts.

Look with compassion on all
who find it difficult to live
with unfulfilled promises
and incompleted obligations
to those whom they love,
and from whom they are now separated
by the gate of death.
Relieve them of their guilt.
Enable them to live with their feelings,
knowing that we all
are gathered together in your love,
whether in this world or the next,
and accepted through your son,
Jesus Christ our Lord.

ACCEPTANCE ▨

I
T is a humbling experience to be told by someone that they know they are dying, and that they would like you to take their funeral when the time comes. So please, could we talk about the service together.

This has happened to me twice in the last few months. In the first instance, June was a patient who had been undergoing prolonged treatment for cancer. She knew that the treatment had come to an end, and that nothing more medically could be done for her except to control the pain and make her as comfortable as possible. With understandable sadness, but with great fortitude and remarkable equanimity, she began to put her affairs in order, and to express her wishes to her family and various other people, including myself.

By contrast, I knew Sylvia as a neighbour in our small corner of south-east London, but the circumstances of her illness were similar to those of June. When she came home from hospital for the last time, she rang me and we fixed a time when I could go round to see her and talk about the details of her funeral which she wanted me to take.

Neither June nor Sylvia was a religious person. June had begun life as an Anglican but had moved away at an early stage. Sylvia had followed suit later in life. Her funeral was not strongly religious. June's was overtly secular. Yet both ceremonies were entirely authentic, and provided a valid vehicle for the many friends and relatives who attended to pay their tributes, say their farewells, and take leave of the two women they had known and loved.

June and Sylvia are people whom I shall always remember, for the strength of their personalities, and for the influence which they had on so many people, including myself. Above all, I shall remember them because they looked death in the eye. They accepted it, and in doing so they overcame it and took away its power.

With this great cloud of witnesses around us, therefore, we too must . . . run with resolution the race which lies ahead of us, our eyes fixed on Jesus, the pioneer and perfecter of faith.   (Hebrews 12: 1–2)

Almighty God,
Ever three, yet ever one,
Perfect in unity,
Source of all truth.

We give thanks to you
for the integrity of all your people,
who use the wisdom and insight
you have given them
to find meaning in life
and acceptance of death.

We thank you
for what we have shared with them,
and our memories of them.

We pray that strengthened
by their good example,
and by our faith in the risen Lord,
we too may face death with confidence,
and overcome its power,
after the pattern of your Son,
Jesus Christ our Lord.

PEACE ▧

THERE is not much peace in hospital. During the day wards are a hive of activity with all kinds of people coming and going on an endless variety of errands. Patients themselves are often on the move, to theatre for surgery, or to various clinics for tests, treatments, and examinations.

At night, it can be difficult to sleep. The ward is not often really quiet, and one restless person can keep everyone else awake. When I was a patient I was woken up in the small hours by a slightly disorientated patient. He wanted to go home, and because the nurses would not let him leave, he became very angry, and verbally abused them. Many wards have a rest period during the middle of the day. Blinds are drawn, activity ceases, and no one is allowed on to the ward for an hour or so.

Inner peace can also be difficult to achieve. There are so many uncertainties in hospital—operations being postponed, appointments cancelled, waiting for the results of tests, the anxieties surrounding diagnosis, the recovery from surgery, the outcome of medical treatment.

The ability to make known the presence of God amongst so many distractions, whether physical or emotional, is one of the essentials of the hospital ministry. Sometimes this will be achieved through the administration of the sacraments. 'I feel better for that,' one of my 'regulars' used to say when I had given him Holy Communion. Sometimes it will be through moments of shared insight, prayer, or simply by holding someone's hand in silence. By whatever means it may be, our contribution to hospital life is to be agents of 'the peace of God which is beyond all understanding'.

Peace is my parting gift to you, my own peace, such as the world cannot give. Set your troubled hearts at rest, and banish your fears.   (John 14: 27)

The peace of God, which is beyond all understanding, will guard your hearts and your thoughts in Christ Jesus.   (Philippians 4: 7)

———————

God our Father,
you are beyond our comprehension
and our knowing,
yet present with us always.

Give to us,
who minister in your name,
the gifts that we need,
peace within ourselves,
and compassion for your people.
Guard their hearts and thoughts
in Christ Jesus,
and grant to them your peace
which is beyond all understanding.

TWO-WAY MINISTRY ▨

Nот long ago, I was a patient in Guy's for an operation. On the morning I was admitted, I was sitting in the side-room which the ward sister had very kindly allotted me. A lady put her head round the door, and expressed surprise at seeing me there. She was even more surprised to know I was a patient—she thought I was just sitting down having a rest! I had come to know her over the previous weeks when her husband had been seriously ill in the intensive care unit. As he recovered, he had been transferred back to the ward, which was the same one to which I had been admitted for surgery. She and her daughter both came to see me regularly, just as I had visited them on ICU.

Another visitor I had was Mary. She had been a patient for a long time, and was one of my regular communicants. The crowning moment was when we met in the corridor, each holding our drainage bags, and discussed with great interest the colour of their respective contents!

These two visitors—and the many members of staff who came to see me or sent me get-well wishes—were a salutary reminder that ministry is a two-way process. It is so easy for those of us who are paid to care to feel that we are the ones who must always be giving. It is good to discover that we can also receive—and without feeling guilty. Surely there are times when it is just as blessed to receive as to give.

The Son of Man did not come to be served but to serve, and to give his life as a ransom for many. (Matthew 20: 28)

A number of women were also present . . . who had all followed him and looked after him. (Mark 15: 40–1)

———————

Father
we give thanks
for the ministry of your son
to all those in need,
and for the women
who followed him,
and looked after his needs.

Grant to us all
who minister in your name,
openness of heart,
so that we may rejoice
to receive the ministry of others
in our time of need.
As members together
of the Body of Christ,
may we know the blessings
of giving and receiving
in the name of your son,
Jesus Christ our Lord.

OTHER FAITHS, OTHER CULTURES ▣

I RECEIVED a call to the children's intensive care unit. Would I go and say prayers for a newly born child who had just been admitted and was critically ill. I reached the Unit and discovered that the child was Muslim. Just at that moment his father arrived. I sought his reassurance that he wanted me, a Christian priest, to say prayers for his son. He assured me that he did, otherwise he would not have asked for me to be called, and intimated that he would like me to offer prayers without further delay. I did so in terms that I hoped would be acceptable to a Muslim. As I finished, the father stooped down, and touched my shoe with his hand. I felt embarrassed, and asked him why he had made that gesture. 'You are a holy man,' he replied. 'We revere you and we honour Jesus as a prophet. We all worship the same God.' It was not the time or the place to get into discussion about issues of comparative religion. The simple statement of belief by this Muslim in great anxiety for his son, and his acceptance of me, seemed sufficient at that moment to span the divide between our respective faiths.

It is interesting that I found that situation easier to deal with than some of the expressions of Christianity which are heavily influenced by local outlook or culture. For example, I found it difficult to take part in a charismatic evangelical funeral for a child who had died in distressing circumstances. The tenor of the whole service was praise, thanksgiving, and celebration. To me this seemed unreal. I appreciate that people need to be positive in their bereavement, but in this instance the sense of loss seemed to have been ignored. Any notion of pain or distress had been banished. It was simply not mentioned or allowed to intrude.

Again, I felt I had nothing to contribute to the keening of a West African family on the ward following the death of a member of their family. They were Christians, but at that moment were expressing their grief and sorrow in their own way and through the medium of their own culture which I could not enter. I could only feel sad for them at a distance.

Father,
you have created us for yourself
and in your own image.
Give us grace to accept ourselves
as we are,
and for what we are.
Make us aware
of our shortcomings,
the boundaries of our culture,
and the limitations of our faith.

Open our inner being
to the expression of other cultures,
and the claims of other faiths,
so that we may perceive them
with broader and wider vision.
May we see that you are above all,
and in all and through all,
and be content that this is so,
for all greatness and goodness are yours,
now and for ever.

THOSE WHO MAKE MISTAKES ◈

I N January 1991 a nurse was accused in court of causing the death of a child left in her care on night duty by wrongly connecting an oxygen tube to the child's arm. She was acquitted of the charge of manslaughter.

In another case which was not the subject of an official inquiry, and never came before the courts, a member of staff misread a prescription, 'moved' the decimal point, and administered ten times the appropriate amount of the drug prescribed.

Even in the best-run hospitals, incidents like these can and do happen. There are all sorts of reasons. Staff may be tired and short-handed, working under stress and the pressure of events. Sometimes genuine accidents—however we describe or define them—do occur. No system can be guaranteed to be completely and absolutely foolproof. Mistakes are made from time to time. In such instances, there is much distress amongst hospital staff and much anger and recrimination on the part of patients and their families.

All of us go wrong again and again.   (James 3: 3)

> Forgive us the wrong we have done,
> as we have forgiven those who have wronged us.
>
> (Matthew 6: 12)
> To err is human, to forgive, divine.
>
> (Alexander Pope)

Father,
look upon us in your mercy.
Forgive us the mistakes we make
through errors of judgement
                inexperience
                lack of knowledge
                our unwillingness to be advised.
Grant us honesty, humility,
and openness of heart and mind,
so that we may learn
through our mistakes,
and the better serve you,
and others for your sake.

A PRAYER OF DEDICATION ▣

ON 13 February 1991 Her Majesty Queen Elizabeth
the Queen Mother paid an official visit to Ronald
McDonald House at Guy's Hospital. The House had been
built by public donations, large and small, in order to provide
accommodation for parents and families of children being treated
in the Evelina Children's Unit in Guy's Hospital.

The following prayer was used at the official visit, and is
included as a suggested pattern for similar occasions in other
hospitals and hospices.

> Lord God our Father,
> the author and giver of all good things,
> we give thanks to you
> for all your great gifts towards us.
>
> We thank you for the goodness
> of the world around us,
> and that you have called us your people
> to share in the work of your creation.
>
> We thank you for all
> who shared the vision
> of the building of this House.
> We give thanks for energy and enthusiasm,
>   skill and experience,
> and we give thanks for all,
> who by their work in many ways,
> brought this project to a successful conclusion.

Father,
we ask your blessing on this House.

We pray that all who stay here
may find it a place of compassion,
peace, and hope.
We pray that all who work here
may give themselves in love.
May they know themselves to be sustained
and renewed day by day
by that love which you have made known to us
in and through your Son,
Jesus Christ our Lord.

In the name of God
and to his glory
we dedicate Ronald McDonald House
in the name of the Father, and of the Son,
and of the Holy Spirit.

III

HOSPITAL STAFF

NURSES ◈

T HE nurses are wonderful. They look after you so well.'
This tribute to the nursing staff is often expressed to me
by patients on the wards. Sometimes the words carry a
rider: 'They're never off their feet. They're always short-staffed.
They're overworked and underpaid.' I have no doubt that the
appreciative comments are genuine, but my guess is that in making
them, patients—and often relatives—are making unconscious
identifications with the younger members of their family or with
people that they know. It could be their own son or daughter,
grandson or granddaughter, looking after them. 'Young people are
not all bad. The papers should get in here and have a look at these
youngsters.'

People may also be projecting on to the nurses their own need
for perfection and certainty in the treatment they receive. They do
not expect things to go wrong or any mistakes to be made. 'It's my
first day in charge,' a recently promoted staff nurse said to me.
'Everything is chaotic.' I assured her that as far as I could see, the
ward was functioning as smoothly and efficiently as it usually did.
But her anxieties were high at that moment, knowing that she was
responsible during that shift not only for the physical care of
patients, but for their emotional needs, their relatives, and the
whole network of ward organization.

Perhaps it remains true that people enter the nursing profession
because they want to care for people, and because they are
primarily attracted by the practical hands-on approach.
Psychological insights and managerial skills have to be acquired
through training and experience. The nurse to whom I was talking
doubted her own competence in these directions. These doubts
were groundless since I had worked with her previously in

situations where she had demonstrated that she had a good grasp of insight and organizational ability. Every nurse has to link professional skills with personal confidence in using them. In this way nurses are able to deliver the standard of whole-person care which patients need and on which their families depend.

Lord Jesus Christ,
we read that your needs were met
during your ministry among us
by those closest to you.

We give thanks for all who are nurses,
for their natural gifts,
for their training,
and for the skills they have acquired.

Grant to nurses, in all areas of their work,
the gifts of sensitivity, perception
and understanding,
both of other people and of themselves.
As those who are closest to patients,
enable them with confidence
to meet all their needs,
physical, emotional, and spiritual,
to care for their whole person,
and to quicken the progress
of healing within them.
We ask this for your name's sake.

MIDWIVES ▣

A MIDWIFE must be able to give the necessary supervision, care, and advice to women during pregnancy, labour, and the postpartum period, to conduct deliveries on her own responsibility and to care for the newborn and the infant . . . She has an important task in health counselling and education, not only for the patients, but also within the family and the community. The work should involve antenatal education and preparation for parenthood and extends to certain areas of gynaecology, family planning and child care . . .' (United Kingdom Central Council for Nursing, *Midwifery and Health Visiting: A Midwife's Code of Practice*, March 1991)

This wide-ranging, but prosaic, official definition was rendered more succinctly and attractively by Gill Aston, a midwifery teacher at Guy's: 'Midwives are in a unique position to enhance the experience of pregnancy, childbirth, and family beginnings for all those most intimately involved.' That short sentence is alive with the feelings of wonder and privilege at being involved in such a poignant moment in people's lives.

Yet when one talks to midwives, one may pick up the feeling that they regard themselves as undervalued and sometimes lacking the professional recognition accorded more readily to their nursing colleagues. This may have something to do with the nature of their work. Although there are now a few male midwives, the vast majority are women, working with and for women, in many instances acting as their advocate and adviser during pregnancy and childbirth. In a real sense they are identified with the secondary status of women in our male-dominated society, and this is an additional burden for them to bear, alongside those inevitably associated with their work. The possibility always exists of the mother's labour turning out to be more difficult than had been anticipated, making great demands on the midwife's professional judgement and expertise. There may be also the risk of unexpected, congenital abnormality, or even stillbirth. Because of the close identification between the midwife and the mother whom she is delivering, and because of the basic expectation that things will go right, the resultant trauma for the midwife when things do go wrong is even greater.

This kind of pressure on midwives is at last being recognized, and the profession is doing its best to offer the understanding and support which are so necessary for its members.

God sent his Son, born of a woman.   (Galatians 4: 4)

Heavenly Father,
when the infant Christ was born among us
he was wrapped in swaddling clothes
and lain in a manger,
because there was no room at the inn.

We give thanks to you
for the work of all midwives,
for their professional skill in the care of mothers,
for their wisdom in understanding family relationships,
and for the love and affection
which they bring to their work.

Be present to bless them in all that they do.
Grant them strength of body,
direction of purpose,
good judgement in their decisions,
and the support which they need.
Help them to know that they share
in your work of creation for your people
and that, as you uphold them in your love,
they are valued in your sight;
through Jesus Christ, our Lord.

DOCTORS ▨

A FORMER patient paid tribute to his surgeon in these words: 'Six years ago, almost to the day, Alan Yates was holding my heart in his hands. My operation had begun by ten o'clock, but it was not the first of Alan's morning. Already he'd mended a hole-in-the-heart of a baby girl, a mite about the size of a small brown loaf. When my wife left the intensive care ward at ten-thirty that night, Alan was still there . . .'

The dramatic nature of the heart surgeon's work and its prospect of spectacular and immediate success, would seem to be full of dangers for the surgeon's soul and, indeed, for his ultimate worth as a doctor. This enormous power in his hands to set the patients down on the edge of eternity, to take the heart out of the body, to cut it and trim it, sew it and rebuild it and put it back in place, restored to fully working order—surely feats like that must make a man feel too much like a god. Must it not take, not only the boldness and skill, but some arrogance too? Working on that tightrope between life and death obviously needs a cool head—but might it not also need a certain hardness of heart? . . . [Yet] you cannot be a good doctor without pity.   (Trevor Philpott, a personal tribute to Alan Yates, Guy's Hospital Chapel, March 1991)

There lies the dilemma. The tension between professional detachment ('some arrogance . . . a certain hardness of heart') and genuine human compassion ('pity') exerts constant tension on physicians and surgeons alike. They are not confronting theoretical issues or academic questions, but people with real anxieties and problems, ultimately about life and death.

One junior doctor wrote: 'I am expected to keep an even temperament when dealing with a whole range of issues in one day. For example, I see patients requesting termination of pregnancy perhaps for the fifth or sixth time, and then patients whose life is ruined by infertility. I see a woman who has miscarried and go from her to deliver a baby on the labour ward. I then hear of parents who have battered their newborn baby to death. I see a patient who has had numerous pregnancies terminated, followed by some live births, who requested sterilization, then requested that sterilization to be reversed and became pregnant. Now she is requesting termination and a repeat sterilization.'

He added other poignant memories that he remembers vividly: 'The husband and two young children whose mother had just died of cancer; the five-year-old burnt in a fire, whom I tried so hard to resuscitate and whom I saw later with an awful prognosis on the intensive care unit; the ninety-year-old man to whom I had to break the news that his eighty-five-year-old wife had died; the couple who had years of infertility and whose baby died at twenty-seven weeks' gestation . . . There are many occasions such as these where one has to walk away from the situation with tears brimming.'

However, being a doctor brings much positive satisfaction: 'I have yet to see anything in life that can match the joy and happiness that you give to a mother and father on handing them their newborn infant . . . The rewards outweigh the problems. For me it is a vocation . . .' (Paul Carter, Registrar in Obstetrics and Gynaecology, Guy's Hospital, 1991).

> **Father almighty,**
> **whose Son was the divine physician,**
> **and numbered among his disciples**
> **Luke the beloved doctor;**
> **we give thanks to you**
> **for all who share your own work**
> **in the practice of medicine.**

We thank you
for the skills they have learned
    the science they apply
    the wisdom they have gained.

We pray that you will sustain them
as they work long hours,
        experience many stresses,
        take great decisions,
        and hold life and death in their hands.
Enable them to use
all the gifts you have given them
for the relief and healing
of your people in their need.
We ask this for your name's sake.

PARAMEDICAL STAFF ◈

DOCTORS and nurses are in the forefront of the generally accepted view of hospital care. But their work would be much less effective without the support and co-operation of members of staff belonging to a number of other disciplines, each making an essential contribution to the total care of the patient.

Physiotherapists provide exercise and movement to hasten recovery. Occupational therapists plan and manage rehabilitation. Dietitians provide special food for patients with eating or digestive difficulties. Pharmacists supervise and advise on medication prescribed for patients. Speech therapists work with people whose powers of speech have been impaired through surgery or strokes. Chiropodists treat people whose feet are causing problems. Medical and psychiatric social workers deal with every kind of personal, domestic, and social problem.

All these people in their various disciplines are included under the heading of paramedical staff. They do not usually receive great acclaim but they form an essential part of hospital care. No hospital could adequately treat its patients without their skill and expertise.

A body is not a single organ, but many.   (I Corinthians 12: 14)

Each of us has been given a special gift, a particular share in the bounty of Christ.   (Ephesians 4: 7)

Gracious God,
you are the source
of all our gifts.

We thank you
for the work of all paramedical staff
in our hospitals.
We thank you
for the wide variety
of their gifts, skill, and expertise.
We thank you
for the contribution they make
to the overall care
of people in hospital.

We pray that you will
prosper their work,
deepen their insight,
increase their knowledge,
and widen their expertise.
As they grow in your gifts,
may they grow as people
and know that in serving others,
they are serving you.

THOSE WHO TEACH AND
THOSE WHO LEARN ◈

A s soon as one enters Guy's Hospital, one is struck by the large number of young people on site. A second glance will confirm that many of them are students. They are studying for qualifications in a wide range of disciplines— medicine, dentistry, nursing, midwifery, physiotherapy, radiography, to name but a few.

Some are continuing their training in pursuit of higher qualifications. Others are attached to Guy's for various lengths of time as part of a training scheme or to gain experience in their own particular discipline. People come to Guy's from all over the world to further and enhance their professional skills.

For staff already in post, there is a wide range of courses, study days, seminars, and workshops. These are designed to provide in-service training, to update and widen professional skills, and to keep abreast of latest thinking and developments in a particular discipline or area of concern. To their number, from time to time I add courses for theological students, in order for them to gain insight into the working of the hospital, and relate what they see and experience to the theology which they learn academically.

Sometimes I feel everyone in Guy's is teaching everyone else. Perhaps that is as it should be. It can only be for the good. Education is, and must be, a shared activity, and there is an equal degree of responsibility on those who teach and those who learn. Ultimately, this is for the good of everyone in hospital, patients, their relatives, and staff alike.

Heavenly Father,
we give thanks for all who teach
and for all who learn in our hospitals.
May those who teach
do so with skill and imagination,
imparting knowledge, and encouraging discovery.
May those who learn
do so with commitment, application,
and openness to all that is new.
Together may they learn from each other
and from you,
source of all knowledge and truth,
to the glory of your name,
and the good of your people in their need.

HOSPITAL MANAGERS ▨

O NE of the great changes I have been aware of over the years is the way in which hospitals are run. When I first became a hospital chaplain, there was a House Governor or Hospital Secretary, a Deputy, an Assistant, and two to three people in the hospital office. There were, of course, all the other departments, Finance, Personnel, Works, and so on, but everything seemed to funnel back through 'the office', where, with a minimum of staff, everything seemed to be attended to, and things seemed to get done.

Even after the major reorganizations of 1974 and the creation of Health Districts, it was still possible to find one's way around the system. One Health District was organized much the same as another, and the administrative structure was reasonably uniform, although functions of a post-holder of the same name could vary from one Health District to another.

All that has changed. Administrators are now managers, and management has been passed down through the organization so the responsibility for decision-making takes place as near as possible to the ward or department concerned. As the holder of a very small chaplaincy budget, I have managerial responsibilities, not onerous, but which have to be dealt with and attended to as efficiently as possible and within a reasonable time-span.

With so many people involved in the process, good management is now more than ever the way to the smooth and efficient functioning of the hospital, and the most effective use of its scarce resources. Ultimately, this can only be for the good of those who come in need of care and treatment.

There are varieties of gifts, but the same Spirit.   (1 Corinthians 12: 4)

———————

Father,
we thank you
for the gifts you have given to us,
and rejoice
in their rich diversity.

May your Holy Spirit
guide and direct
all those who work
as managers
in our hospitals.
Grant them your gifts of orderliness,
                              efficiency,
                              communication,
                              right judgement,
so that all hospital staff
may be enabled
to work with one another
more closely,
more efficiently,
and with more understanding
of the needs of those who come
to hospital for treatment,
and to care more effectively for them.
We ask this for your name's sake.

ANCILLARY STAFF ◈

SOMETIMES, in odd moments, I wonder which is the most important department of the hospital. I usually end with a dead heat between catering, the boiler-room, and the laundry. I have a vivid recollection of a charge nurse trying to work out how he would divide a delivery of twenty pairs of clean knickers between thirty elderly and incontinent female patients. Without the provision of everyday facilities such as food, laundry, cleaning, portering, and the maintenance of buildings, it is impossible for a hospital to function.

Many such staff never come near the patients at all, yet patients rely heavily upon them, and upon the efficient discharge of their duties. Much of the work is inevitably tedious and repetitive. Yet it has to be done. It is important that the staff who do it should not be overlooked or taken for granted. They need to feel—and rightly so—that they are valued because they have a vital part to play in the life of the hospital.

> Father in heaven,
> your Son shared the life
> of an earthly home,
> and worked each day
> by the skill of his hands
> in the carpenter's shop.
>
> We give you thanks
> for those who, by their work
> in many areas
> sustain the life of our hospitals,
> and the care of those who are patients.

May all who depend upon them
accord them value as people,
and esteem for what they do,
after the pattern of your Son,
Jesus Christ our Lord.

HOSPITAL CHAPLAINS ▣

Many years ago, I sent out a circular to all the wards. I have long forgotten what it was about but to me, at least, it must have been an important subject. A day or two later I went up to one of the wards where sister had papers clipped neatly together on her desk. One clip was marked 'Action'. A second was marked 'Non-urgent'. The third was marked 'Odds and Bods'. There, on the third clip, was my precious circular! It indicated to me immediately my place in the hospital order of things, at least as that sister perceived it.

A chaplain can react in two ways to that kind of situation. It is possible to protest, to defend one's position, and probably endanger good relationships in doing so. Or it is possible to say that it is not necessarily a bad thing to be at the bottom of the pile. First, it is scriptural. Jesus warned his disciples that this is what would happen to them. Secondly, when one is at the bottom of the pile, the only possible direction in which to move is upwards. And thirdly, it can be a positive advantage to have no designated place within the institution, no 'grading' within the hospital hierarchy. Thus chaplains have access to every level of staff, from cleaners to consultants.

That is not to say, however, that chaplains have no place within the hospital. Their position is established and, at a time when hospitals are becoming increasingly holistic in their approach to patient care, chaplains have a place in the prevailing culture. Nevertheless, the place has to be earned, and recognition has to be won. Chaplains have to prove that they have a contribution to make to the care of patients, relatives, and staff. Once they have crossed this threshold, the scope of their work is virtually boundless, and their ministry is welcomed. The apathy and indifference of many people is directed towards the institutional churches rather than to the Gospel itself. Chaplains work in a secular setting on the frontiers between the Christian faith and the world it professes to love and care for. They seek to make explicit the Good News which is implicit in their presence within the hospital. By doing so, they forward God's healing purposes for his people.

Calling the Twelve together, [Jesus] . . . sent them out to proclaim the kingdom of God and to heal the sick.   (Luke 9: 1–2)

Lord Jesus Christ,
you sent out your disciples
to proclaim the Kingdom,
and to heal the sick in your name.

We give thanks to you
for all who work as hospital chaplains.
May your word be a lamp to their feet,
and a light to their paths,
so that, in serving others,
they may follow you.

By word, sacrament, and example,
may they make your presence known
to those in their care.
Grant them strength of body,
        depths of compassion,
        and firmness of faith,
so that they may meet the demands laid upon them
in your name
in sure trust in your love.

VOLUNTEERS ◩

MR GUY'S hospital was opened in 1725 for the care of the incurable and the insane. Guy was one of the governors of St Thomas's which stood across the street, and had leased the land from that hospital at his own expense. St Thomas's itself was an ancient Christian foundation, which, together with St Bartholomew's in Smithfield, was a forerunner of the many hospitals which were founded under Church auspices or through Church initiatives down the years, especially during the Victorian era.

The twin principles of philanthropy and voluntary work have always been strong in the hospital world. A relative of mine, with ample financial means, worked for many years as a ward sister in a major hospital without taking any payment for her services. Many towns and cities ran their 'penny-a-week' fund for their local hospital or convalescent home, and some still maintain the observance of their 'Hospital Sunday'.

When the National Health Service was established in the United Kingdom, it appeared that the voluntary principle was being dispensed with. The state could and should pay for all that was needed. It soon became apparent that this was far from being the case. Hospitals were glad to welcome the support of leagues of Friends and informal groups who raised money to buy specific and expensive items of equipment which were beyond the hospital budget. Voluntary Services Organizers were appointed to oversee and co-ordinate the specific contribution which volunteers could make towards maintaining the life of the hospital, and developing the facilities provided: trolley shops, cafeterias, flowers, hair-dressing, manicures, manning information desks, directing and escorting patients through the maze of corridors, and so on. All these areas of activity help to promote the 'human' face of the hospital for which, all too often, there is insufficient time, money, or, unfortunately, motivation.

It is impossible to quantify the contribution which volunteers make to hospital life, but without them it would be short of many amenities which add significantly to the care and comfort of both patients and staff.

Truly I tell you: anything you did for one of my brothers here . . . you did for me.   (Matthew 25: 40)

Jesus said: I am among you like a servant.   (Luke 22: 27)

Father,
we give thanks for all those
who use the gifts, time, and talents
that you have given them
in the service of our hospitals
without seeking payment in return.

Prosper their work
on behalf of those who are ill.
Use them in your service.
Enrich them with the knowledge
that in ministering to others,
they are ministering to you
after the pattern of Jesus, your Son,
who came not to be served but to serve
and to give his life for us all;
who now lives and reigns with you
in the unity of the Spirit,
God for evermore.

INDEX ◈